How to get on in **Marketing**

How to get on in Marketing

A Career Development Guide

Third Edition

Edited by
Norman A. Hart, MSc, FCAM, FInst.M, FIPR
and
Norman E. Waite, MSc, DMS, DipM, MInst.M, Cert.Ed.

Published in consultation with
CAM Foundation and the Institute of Marketing

Kogan Page

First published in Great Britain as
A Career in Marketing, Advertising and Public Relations
by William Heinemann Ltd 1981
Second edition 1985
(ISBN 0 434 90711 1)
Third edition published 1987 by
Kogan Page Ltd, 120 Pentonville Road, London N1

Reprinted 1988

British Library Cataloguing in Publication Data

How to get on in marketing, advertising and
public relations. —— 3rd ed.
1. Marketing —— Vocational guidance ——
Great Britain
I. Hart, Norman A. II. Waite, Norman
658.8'0023'41 HF5415.12.G7

ISBN 1-85091-354-4

Printed in Great Britain by
Biddles Ltd, Guildford

Contents

Biographical Notes

Professor Michael J. Baker, TD, BA, BSc(Econ), DBA, DipM, FInstM, FCAM

Professor Baker has been head of the Department of Marketing at Strathclyde University since its inception in 1971. After graduation (BA, Durham) and military service, he spent six years in the steel industry selling flat-rolled products, followed by four years in further education as a lecturer in Marketing. He attended Harvard Business School as a Foundation for Management Education Fellow 1968–71 and was awarded a doctorate in Business Administration. He is the author/editor of eleven books including *Marketing New Industrial Products* (1975), *Product Policy and Management* (with R. McTavish, 1976), *Offshore Inspection and Maintenance* (with S. T. Parkinson and M. A. Saren, 1978), *Industrial Innovation* (ed., 1979), *Market Development* (1983), *Marketing Theory and Practice* (2nd edition 1983), *Marketing Strategy and Management* (1985) and *Marketing* (4th edition 1985), the most widely-used UK text on the subject. He has extensive consulting experience in the areas of marketing strategy and new product development.

Roderick Braithwaite, MA(Cantab), MCAM, FIPA

Chief Executive of Charles Barker Human Resources, one of the leading recruitment organizations in the UK, Roderick Braithwaite read Law and Modern Languages at Queen's College, Cambridge, and is the author of the industry's research study, *Communications and the Job-Seeker* and of *How to Recruit* published by the British Institute of Management. He is a frequent contributor, as a writer and speaker, on a wide range of recruitment and careers guidance topics.

Norman A. Hart, MSc, FCAM, FIPR, FInstM

Managing Director of International Limited, Norman Hart was previously Director of the CAM Foundation. He joined Roles & Parker Limited in 1957 and was Group Chief Executive when he left to become Publicity Manager of a Unilever company, Thames Board Mills. He subsequently became Marketing Manager and finally went into publishing with Morgan Grampian, where he was Divisional General Manager. A frequent speaker on advertising, public relations and marketing, both in the UK and overseas, Mr Hart is the author of a number of books, including *Practical Advertising and Publicity*. He is also a Visiting Fellow of the University of Bradford and holds a Master's Degree in Management Studies.

Roger Hayes, BSc(Hons), MCAM

Roger Hayes is Director of Corporate Communications with Thorn EMI. He was previously a director of Burson-Marsteller Limited, one of the largest public relations consultancies in the UK, and was also a Vice-President of Burson-Marsteller International, the second largest PR consultants in the world. He entered communications in 1966 as a Young & Rubicam advertising agency trainee before moving into journalism with Reuters, first as a London-based city reporter and later as an economics correspondent in Paris. He has over a decade of experience in public relations. A specialist in public affairs and international accounts, he has conducted a variety of campaigns for governments, UK, Japanese and European companies, financial institutions and associations in the UK and overseas. He writes and lectures frequently on Public Relations training and education, and is a member of an international commission on communications education.

Gilbert W Lamb, DipCAM

Gilbert Lamb was born in 1924 and educated at Clifton College, following which he served in the Grenadier Guards from 1942 until 1962 when he retired with the rank of major. In 1954 he attended the Staff College at Camberley and in 1962 was called to the Bar as a member of Grays Inn. In the same year he joined Formica Limited, part of the De La Rue Group, as a Sales Manager. Two years later he set up a Marketing Company for Formica Limited in Switzerland and from 1965 until 1968 he was the Chief Executive for Formica India Limited in Poona. The following two years saw him as Managing Director of Formica Limited in England, during which time he attended a two-month executive programme at Stamford University, California. From 1971 until 1979 he was Director of The Incorporated Society of British Advertisers Limited (ISBA), becoming a DipCAM in 1976 and being appointed to the CBI Committee on Marketing and Consumer Affairs in 1978. He left ISBA to become Director of Communication and Public Affairs for the TI Group, and subsequently has set up as a private consultant.

Patricia Mann FCAM, FIPA

Patricia Mann is Head of External Affairs of the JWT Group, Vice President, J. Walter Thompson International and Editor of *Consumer Affairs*, sponsored by the JWT Group. Since 1983, she has also been a Director of the Woolwich Equitable Building Society. She is a Council Member of the Advertising Standards Authority, the Institute of Practitioners in Advertising, the European Association of Advertising Agencies and Brunel University. She is a member of the Court of Governors of Henley — the Management College, Chairman of the Advertising Consumer Liaison Group, and was for seven years a Governor of CAM. She is the author of *150 Careers in Advertising*, (Longmans, 1971).

Richard N Skinner, BA, FInstM

Educated at Brentwood School and University College, London, where he read Classics, Richard Skinner spent his first ten years in marketing with Remington Rand Limited, moving from direct selling, through sales training and field management, to product management and market research. He joined Reliance Systems Limited as Sales Manager in 1964 and became Deputy Managing Director. His publications include *Launching New Products in Competitive Markets*, *Organizing for Marketing on a Small Budget*, *How British Industry Prices* and *Pricing Strategies to Cope with Inflation*. He has lectured on selling and marketing topics to a variety of organizations including BIM, IEE, the Japanese Marketing Association, CAM and the Institute of Marketing, of which he is a Fellow. He is now a private consultant.

Norman E Waite, MSc, DMS, DipM, MInstM, Cert.Ed.

Norman Waite is Director of Education at the Institute of Marketing and has been responsible for the professional qualifications courses and examinations since 1980. His work also includes responsibility for careers advice to those who are interested in marketing as a career.

A graduate of the University of Bath, after military service he spent seventeen years in industry with Bestobell Limited and British Gas, holding various marketing management appointments until accepting the post of Senior Lecturer in Business Management at the North Gloucestershire College of Technology, Cheltenham. After seven years of full-time lecturing, during which time he was tutor for the marketing courses, he joined the Institute of Marketing to head up the professional qualifications and education section.

He is a member of the Postgraduate Studies Board of the CNAA, the BTEC Validation Committee and External Examiner on a number of degree and postgraduate Diploma courses — other responsibilities include membership of the Court of the Universities of Lancaster and Stirling. He is Managing Editor of *The Quarterly Review of Marketing* and is co-editor for a book of readings on marketing published by Heinemann.

Christopher J West, BSc (Econ)

Christopher West is chairman of Business Marketing Services Limited, a London-based research and marketing consultancy. He graduated from the London School of Economics and subsequently worked in a variety of research posts for Shell International and Eurofinance, a Paris-based financial and economic consultancy. On returning to the United Kingdom, Chris West became a Director of Industrial Market Research Ltd and was later appointed as Managing Director. Chris West writes and lectures extensively on marketing subjects. He has edited two books — *Marketing on a Small Budget* and *Inflation: A Management Guide to Survival* and has contributed articles to major marketing magazines including the *Harvard Business Review*. He has lectured in the UK, Norway, Sweden, Denmark, Finland, the USA, Singapore, Malaysia and South Africa, primarily for local marketing bodies, but also for business schools and private clients.

David Wheeler, BSc(Econ), FIPA

Director General of the Institute of Practitioners in Advertising since January 1978, David Wheeler was formerly Media Director at J. Walter Thompson Company Limited, Deputy Chairman of the British Market Research Bureau and Joint Managing Director of Portland Outdoor Advertising Limited. Before joining J. Walter Thompson in 1969, he was Managing Director of Television Audience Measurement Limited (TAM) and the associated Attwood/Nielsen television research companies in Ireland and West Germany, and a director of the Attwood Group. Earlier, he was for three years Marketing Controller of Fisons Pharmaceuticals Limited, responsible for their marketing and advertising activities. He is a member of many of the main committees that govern the practice and development of advertising: the Council, Executive Committee and Public Action Group of the Advertising Association; the British Code of Advertising Practice Committee; the European Association of Advertising Agencies' Board of Control; and the joint industries committees for research in press, television, radio and posters. He is a member of the British National Committee of the International Chamber of Commerce in London and also the Council of the CBI.

Introduction

In this book we look at the subject of a career in marketing, advertising and public relations in some detail. We cover education, and how to get started, and then we look at each of the main functions. There are chapters on marketing, selling, advertising, public relations and research. We concentrate on the selling of consumer goods and services, although much of what we say also applies to the other more specialized fields such as financial, recruitment, industrial, international, and so on. We end with a practical chapter setting out possible courses of action for someone considering such a career. The suggestions in this final chapter will certainly not suit everyone but will, we believe, prove a useful guide for the student who, after reading this book, is still uncertain where to begin.

A career in the field of marketing and the many related fields of activity, whether it be angled towards selling, advertising or public relations for instance, provides the scope for a wide range of individual talents. There are opportunities for the person who can write well, or talk well; the person who is good with people; the person with creative talents or an aptitude in numeracy, and the person with an all-round knowledge and experience of commercial life. It is not only the student from a university or polytechnic for whom this book is written, although inevitably the young starter is particularly in mind in the advice given in the chapters of the book. There is much in it that will be of interest to the mature and experienced person who wishes to broaden his commercial experience or, having worked in several of the departments of industry or commerce, now wishes to settle for a career in some field of communications or marketing. The book is also designed to help those in universities and schools who find themselves having to give careers advice to their pupils. We believe it will be particularly useful for such people.

Inevitably, it is impossible to isolate every job-function in the business of marketing, advertising and communications as they are so inter-related. There is therefore some overlap between chapters, particularly as each chapter has been written by an expert in the subject covered. The editors have deliberately left the chapters as originally written, to help those readers who wish to go straight to a chapter rather than start at the beginning and work through to the end of the book.

All of the authors have had wide commercial experience and have held or are holding top jobs in marketing or communications. The reader therefore may feel daunted by the qualities and the requirements which are set out as being necessary for success. We would say, don't be put off. You do not have to be a paragon of a business executive to be successful in any one of the fields covered in the book. Certainly to achieve the top, you must be above average — and that can only be achieved by a few. In describing the qualities needed for success in the branch of marketing covered in a particular chapter, the author has aimed for the ideal. But anyone with integrity, intelligence, common sense, application, and the ability to work hard can succeed in one or other of the marketing disciplines which are explained and discussed in the following pages.

The reader will observe that every chapter in the book mentions the importance of having a recognized qualification. A university degree may well be the best qualification of all, but even a degree is not necessarily sufficient in these days to secure the job you are looking for. A specialist qualification in the particular discipline in which you wish to make your career is also strongly recommended. Certainly there are many successful people who have achieved the highest position without ever passing any examinations. But these are the exceptions and we will see less of them in the future. The student is therefore urged to decide where he wants to go and obtain the right qualification for the job. Beware however of spurious qualifications which carry no weight. Check on the standing of the qualification before enrolling for a course.

We congratulate CAM and the Institute of Marketing in sponsoring this book, and we thank the authors of the various chapters in it. To the reader we say — remember that this book will not make any decisions for you. It will, however, outline the options open to you and give you some advice on how to follow up and learn more about the special field you decide is the right one for you.

While there have been no fundamental changes since the last edition, each chapter has been carefully examined by its respective author, and updated wherever necessary.

The need continues to grow for expert, capable and enthusiastic practitioners in marketing, and with it a perceived need for young entrants to acquire a relevant qualification. Only in this way can we hope to increase wealth for the individuals concerned, their organization, and indeed for the country as a whole.

The outcome, increased sales, is a vital concomitant to increased productivity as one of the means of countering increasing unemployment.

Norman A Hart
Norman E Waite

1. Marketing as a Career

Norman Waite and Gilbert Lamb

Do you see yourself in a job:

- where your activities and decisions will really affect the success of your company
- where you are dealing with the challenge of a rapidly changing business environment
- where you are constantly trying to provide a better product or service to satisfy customer demand
- where you will be well rewarded for your achievements?

Then you should choose marketing as your career.

Marketing

Don't think, as many people still do, that marketing is just the smart 'in' word for selling. Selling is a vital, indispensable component of marketing, but only one of several other activities. Marketing thinking and planning begins at, or even before, the drawing board and ends only when the company has made certain that the customer is really satisfied with the product or service provided.

Marketing is the business function which endeavours to "bring the right goods and services to the consumer in the most efficient and profitable way". The Institute of Marketing's more precise definition is "the management process responsible for identifying, anticipating and satisfying customer requirements profitably".

The marketing function is an essential activity in all business organizations and there are opportunities for people with qualifications in technical, arts and science subjects. There are three broad categories into which this career area is commonly divided, namely Consumer, Industrial and Services marketing.

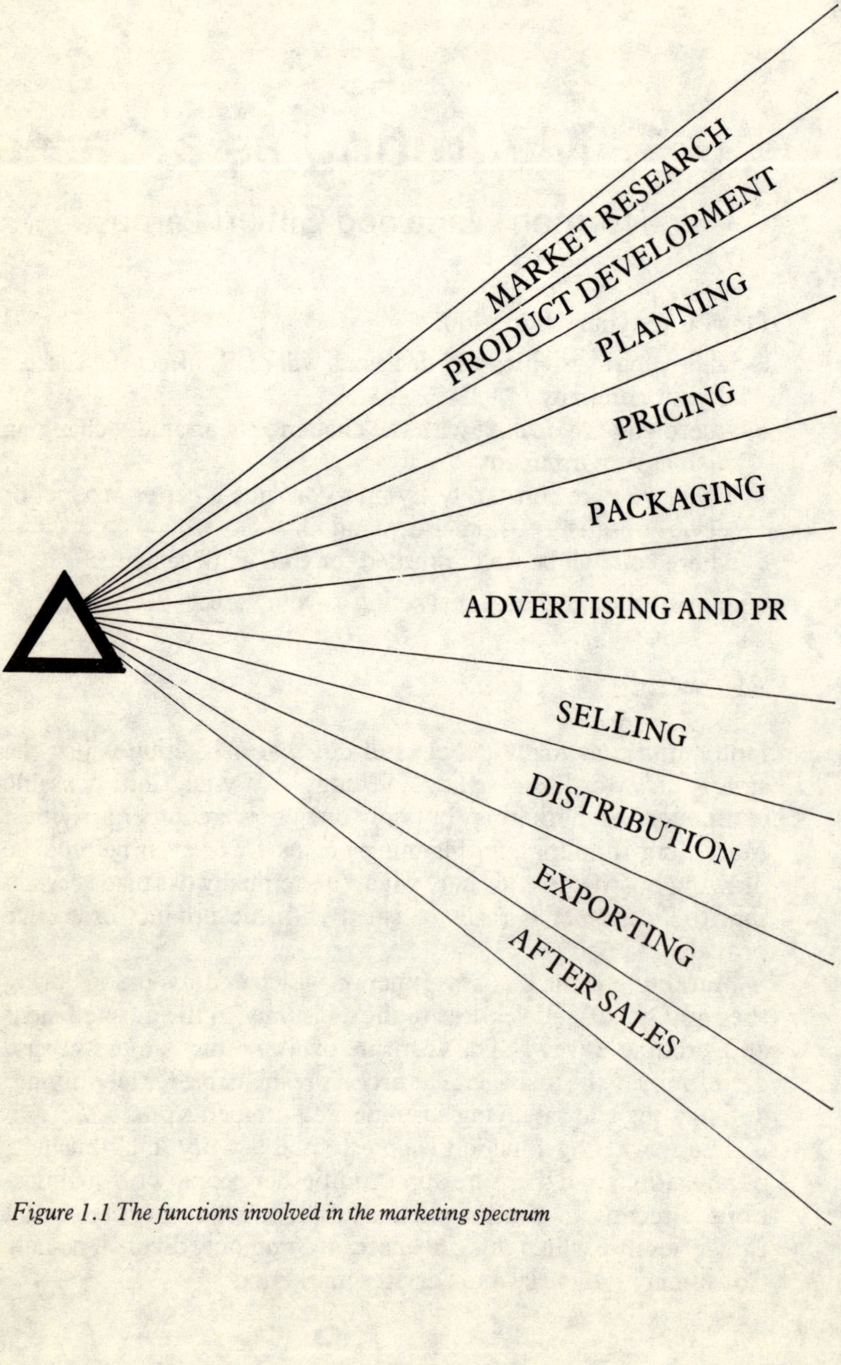

Figure 1.1 The functions involved in the marketing spectrum

Research How accurately can customer needs be forecast? What does the customer really want? How big is the potential market?

Development Can the research findings be converted into a product or service that the customer will buy?

Planning Has the company enough expertise and facilities to make a new product or offer a new service? Will the new product look good and represent good value?

Pricing Is the price right for the target market? What are the competitors charging? What is an adequate profit margin? Could the company reduce its costs?

Packaging Does the product need protection from contamination? Does the pack need to carry instructions for use? Will attractive packaging help to sell the product?

Promotion Which sort of advertising and promotion will best suit the product or service — T.V., radio, national press? Will displays be arranged in shops to 'merchandise' the product? What about public relations — will potential customers be well disposed towards the company and what it is offering?

Sales To whom will the company be selling — to members of the public, wholesalers and retailers? What level of technical knowledge will the sales staff require?

Distribution Is the product to be distributed through the company's own retail outlets or to wholesalers? Could the product be sold direct to the public through mail order catalogues or advertisements? What methods of physical distribution will be used?

Overseas Operations Has the company got people with the specialist knowledge of overseas markets? Do they know all the regulations governing exports to different countries? Will the company use overseas agents? Is there a language barrier for the product to overcome?

After Sales Service Can the company produce supplies of spare parts that the product might require? Will service engineers be available, when necessary, to maintain equipment?

- consumer marketing — which includes all domestic products which are sold mainly through retail outlets
- industrial marketing — where components and products are sold to other industrial companies
- marketing of services — such as banking, insurance, holidays, etc.

A further differentiation may be applied, namely overseas marketing which is really an extension of one of the above categories.

Marketing is a generic term for a wide group of business activities, sometimes referred to as the marketing spectrum (Figure 1.1) whose main objective is to obtain new customers and keep existing ones.

Your Career in Marketing

Because marketing affects so many of the company's resources and activities, it is essentially a team effort. Good marketing is the end product of a well-led management team fully embracing the marketing concept. Marketing executives are responsible for providing the basic information and guidance about prospective markets, their behaviour, size and potential for each product or service within the company. Their role is to promote better marketing throughout the company structure, to draw up the marketing plans and to ensure that these are implemented efficiently and profitably.

To be a real success in marketing you will need to have, or to develop, qualities which are generally agreed to be the essential ingredients of the manager. These will include: intelligence, integrity, courage and enthusiasm, together with the required knowledge to carry out a difficult but immensely rewarding job. Few would disagree that marketing, although one of the most interesting careers today, is challenging and demanding. Markets are constantly changing so that unrelenting energy and a sense of responsibility will be needed throughout.

Marketing, as a profession, offers scope for a large variety of talents, since it requires a grasp of many areas of academic study for successful practice. Wherever your abilities lie, the rewards can be high and immediate. Pay is normally geared to merit.

Employers increasingly recognize the importance and contribution of marketing and many are actively encouraging and assisting promising employees to obtain the marketing qualifications which are essential to today's business environment.

Marketing people emerge as rather special businessmen, broad in outlook and necessarily highly trained by education and experience to use a large armoury of marketing techniques that are often sophisticated and delicate in operation. The outcome of great undertakings in production and distribution depend on their ability and imagination; their plans may require the support of massive investment in productive plant and materials and in costly forms of communication such as advertising and sales force operation. Only those who combine the right personal qualities with a completely professional approach both in preparation and execution of the marketing management role are likely to be entrusted with its substantial responsibilities and to receive the high rewards that it offers in terms of status and remuneration.

Marketing

One result of the longest recession the British economy has suffered in this century has been the realization by everyone of the importance of marketing. Many companies, previously able to sell their products without much effort in a buoyant home market, have realized that if they are to compete with imports and if they are ever to export successfully, marketing must be taken seriously.

There are those who believe that much of the failure of some sections of British industry in the 1960s and 70s was failure of marketing. It may be a truism to say that industry must make what it can sell. There can be few companies in Britain today where anyone, from the managing director to the newest operative, is not aware of the importance of the customer. It is people in marketing, in this case the sales force, who are in direct touch with the customer and who know the market place.

Marketing starts with an evaluation of customer needs and wants, goes on to embrace the design of the product, the branding and packaging, test marketing and the national launch, advertising and promotion, selling, delivery and after-sales service (where applicable). Most of these aspects of marketing are covered in this book. But the book is also about communication and it will become obvious that the marketing person has to be a good communicator. You must be able to find out what the market wants. You must then convey that requirement to the designer, the product developer, the laboratory technician, or the scientist, so that the right product is designed, or so that an existing product is re-developed and improved to meet an established customer requirement. You must be able to explain and justify this requirement at all levels in the enterprise; not only to the managing director and the chief accountant, but also to the production manager and the quality control department. Eventually you must be able to enthuse the sales force and the distributors, both at wholesale and retail level.

In Britain we have achieved an outstanding record for inventions, good ideas and good products. Our greatest failure has been exploiting these; not only at the design stage, but also in our ability to get pricing, distribution, and in particular, delivery and after-sales service right. For too long there has been an attitude that says:

> "It's made in Sheffield/Derby/etc. etc., so it *must* be good."
> "Those foreigners don't know a good product when they see one."
> "We have always made it this way, why should we change?"

In other words we have simply ignored the basic principles of marketing. This leads logically to considering the importance of the export market. Here there are special opportunities for the linguist. Gone are the days when an Englishman could put over what he wanted to say simply by talking loudly. No salesman should go into an export market to sell unless he can speak the language of the country. What hope has a Japanese salesman in England, selling Japanese TV sets, who cannot speak English? Surely the same argument should apply to an Englishman selling whisky in Japan. It does *not* yet apply — but it should, and it will before the end of the next decade. Therefore there is a bright future in industry for the student of languages.

It is however axiomatic that for most products (although there are some notable exceptions) a buoyant home market is a prerequisite for successful exports. For all the importance of export markets to the national economy, the home market will usually generate the essential profits without which no enterprise can exist for long. In this home market the competition from UK and foreign products will be fierce, and once again success will go to the company with the best marketing.

An intrinsic part of marketing, even if sometimes one stage removed, is public affairs and/or public relations, covered in some detail in Chapter 8.

Public Relations

In the past PR has had its detractors but today the good PR person must be as qualified and as professional as the company secretary or the accountant. There is a growing recognition by senior management of the importance of projecting the good news and the achievements of a company to its customers, shareholders, and employees and to the world at large. Just as importantly there must be someone trained and experienced in handling the bad news. The public relations manager therefore has a hugely important task as the guardian of the good name of the enterprise.

With an ever increasing involvement by government and bureaucracy at national and supra-national level, in the day to day affairs of commerce and industry, companies must be fully alert to what is going on. They must know in advance what may, or could, happen because of government legislation or regulation. They need to know how to influence events and who makes decisions or advises on them, at all levels. The work involved in public affairs is therefore detailed and time-consuming. It requires strategic thinking, attention to detail, long-term application and tact.

Public affairs and public relations comprise therefore the external projection of the company, encompassing both the direct association with shareholders, suppliers and customers and the indirect link with national and local government, regional authorities, institutions, trade associations and chambers of commerce, and finally, perhaps most importantly, communications with employees.

We are in a telecommunications revolution taking us into a new age of "telecommuting". This new era is having major consequences for business in general and certainly for marketing. At the same time there is evidence of a move from large factories employing thousands of people to smaller, self-contained units, highly automated and with few employees. Computer assisted design is now a marketing tool which provides new and exciting opportunities for the technical salesman. The changing and the fast developing communications technology is, however, a subject for another book.

Having decided to embark on a career in some branch of communications or marketing you will be wise to equip youself with the necessary qualifications to enable you to go after the job of your choice. First you must know the business you want to go into. Some people will be attracted to an industrial company, others to a company making fast-moving consumer goods or to service industries such as banking, building societies and insurance companies. Others again will prefer to move directly to such specialized operations as advertising agencies, public relations companies, design studios, journalism, research and many other specialities.

That is all very well, you will say, but where do I start? Clearly there are many different openings to consider. Experience in the accounts department is never a waste of time; time on the shop floor is always valuable; but for a marketing man a year or two in sales administration followed by actual experience of selling is vital. The specialist without sales experience is like the general who has never commanded a platoon — however brilliant he may be as a staff officer he doesn't really know what happens at the sharp end. After such experience you will be in a position to decide whether to stay with a manufacturing company or to go to a service company, or again to specialize in a particular sector of commercial activity. You are now ready to survey the business world and to decide where you fit in. The opportunities are enormous.

Before looking at specific areas of marketing it would be sensible to take note of the hardware which is available now, or which will be available very soon. The technological developments of recent years have opened up new opportunities for communication which management must fully utilize.

In this chapter we have looked briefly at the huge and exciting variety offered by a career in marketing and marketing communications. It has opened the door for a glimpse of the many different rooms within. In the following chapters you can enter the central corridor of marketing, look into each room, and assess the demands made and the opportunities offered by a career that begins in that room. You can decide which of the many and various opportunities suits best. Having made this decision it is up to you to land your first job. There is a wealth of good advice in this book, all of it from experts with proven success in their careers. Don't be misled by the detail or depressed by the difficulties. Make your mind up; go hard for what you want; remember that *everyone* has *something* unique to offer — and good luck to you!

2. What Qualifications are Appropriate?

Norman Waite

It is assumed that the majority of readers of this book will currently be pupils or students in the education system. Other readers may already be in work and have decided to pursue their studies on a part-time basis. I have, therefore, included details and advice concerning courses and qualifications appropriate to you all.

School pupils should first and foremost aim to secure a pass in mathematics and English language. (Alternatively, subjects that indicate proficiency in these two important areas may also be acceptable.) Additional passes in other curriculum subjects at GCSE (or equivalent) O-level, according to your ability, are also desirable. The following business related subjects are now available at O-level: economics, law, accounting, statistics and commerce.

Check entry qualifications for any further or higher education course that you may wish to pursue by contacting the appropriate educational institution or professional body. Information should also be available from your local careers adviser.'

GCE A-level subjects should be chosen mainly on the basis of subjects in which you will obtain the highest examination mark. Entry to degree courses at university as well as polytechnics and colleges of higher education, often depend on the candidate scoring a high number of points from their GCE A-level results. Points are scored according to the grade received; for example A=5 points, B=4 points, C=3 points, D=2 points and E=1 point.

This usually means that it is more important to get high grades in your GCE A-levels rather than passes in particular subjects. This is equally applicable to business and/or marketing degrees as any other.

However, all things being equal, GCE A-level subjects such as economics and, where available, business studies, will provide a good background understanding for those contemplating further or higher education courses in marketing or business studies, and are also appropriate for those intending to seek work after leaving school.

A further qualification available to young people in the 16–19 year old age group is the recently introduced "Foundation Certificate in Marketing". This course has been designed for both sixth form students and those on the Youth Training Scheme but at the present time, it is only available at selected schools and YTS centres. This two-year Foundation Certificate in Marketing course is certificated by the Institute of Marketing and is a recognised subject qualification, acceptable for entry to higher level courses at colleges of further and higher education. Practical assignments are a feature of this course and count towards your final result. Passes in this subject also give a subject exemption from the institute's professional certificate course.

Access to further and higher education courses depends on your existing qualifications and, although most courses lead on to other higher level qualifications, this may not always be the case; students are recommended to check on the opportunities that may be open to them to progress to other appropriate or higher level courses once their immediate programme of study has been satisfactorily completed. The newly established National Council for Vocational Qualifications (NCVQ) has this issue as one of its main objectives and the inter-relationship and mutual recognition of the various programmes of vocational study mentioned in this chapter will be developed still further in the future. In the meantime, however, students should plan their further and higher education, including vocational qualifications, with this particular point in mind.

Further education colleges also provide an alternative to the GCE A-level qualification, namely the BTEC National Diploma (or in Scotland the SCOTVEC equivalent) in business studies (ensure that it includes a marketing module) — normal entry requirements are four GCSE (or equivalent) subjects. Successful completion of this course at distinction level can entitle students to apply for entry to a business degree course.

Those who obtain a standard pass at BTEC/SCOTVEC National level, will then be qualified to enrol on the BTEC/ SCOTVEC Higher National Diploma in Business Studies —

students should ensure that the course has a marketing option. BTEC/SCOTVEC courses are offered by most further and higher education colleges, including polytechnics throughout the UK. Although some BTEC courses are available on a part-time basis, it may be more appropriate for students to consider the qualification courses offered by the professional bodies such as the Institute of Marketing, the CAM Foundation, the Market Research Society or the Institute of Export. These courses are usually offered on an evenings-only basis at local further and higher education colleges, as well as through correspondence courses. A list showing the names of colleges which normally offer one or more of these professional courses is shown at the end of this chapter.

The Institute of Marketing is the largest professional body with over 20,000 members and a further 16,000 registered students. Their qualification courses include a Certificate in Sales Management, Certificate in Marketing and a Diploma in Marketing. One or more of these courses are normally available from all the colleges listed.

The CAM Foundation examines for a number of specialist membership bodies concerned with the general area of marketing communications, such as advertising and public relations. A certificate and diploma qualification is also available but courses are run at fewer colleges.

The Market Research Society Diploma is normally only available via a distance learning programme or can be awarded to those who reach an approved standard on certain degree programmes.

The Institute of Export Diploma course is also available from a few of the colleges listed.

Full details of course availability, entry requirements and fees, can be obtained by making direct contact with the appropriate student registration officer of the professional body concerned. Addresses and telephone numbers of these professional bodies are shown at the end of this chapter.

Degree courses in marketing (single or joint honours) or business studies (with a significant marketing input) may accept students who possess the required GCE A-level results, a BTEC national diploma (with distinction) or a BTEC higher national diploma. Courses are offered at universities, polytechnics or colleges of higher education. Universities offer their own degrees whereas the polytechnics and colleges of higher education offer Council for National Academic Awards (CNAA) degrees. A list showing the main universities and colleges which traditionally offer these degree courses are also shown at the end of this chapter. I would hasten to add, however, that the list is not exhaustive and over time new courses are offered and others are changed so you are also advised to refer to annual directories, such as *Which Degree?*, published by Kogan Page. In addition, it is worth writing off for an up-to-date list from the CNAA, 344–354, Gray's Inn Road, London WC1X 8BP.

In the main, you will note that there are only a few specialized first degrees in marketing available, whereas business degrees are fairly commonplace. In choosing a business degree course, you should ensure that you have the opportunity to elect to study marketing as a specialist subject and these can vary from course to course, so endeavour to choose one which suits your particular needs. The CNAA degrees are particularly commended as they are usually sandwich courses and include one year in industry which serves to give students practical business experience and thus enables them to relate theory to practice. At the end of this type of course, it would be legitimate for you to say that you have had one year's work experience — this seems to be a prerequisite for most of the job vacancies which are advertised.

Professional bodies grant various exemptions to marketing students who satisfactorily obtain the BTEC/SCOTVEC higher national diploma and/or a bachelor's degree. For example, the Institute of Marketing exempts HND holders from their two-stage certificate course, enabling students to enter directly onto the one-year diploma programme. Holders of degrees in which marketing has been a specialization can obtain the maximum exemptions. This could mean that the student only has to take the main "case study" (Marketing Management Analysis and Decision) examination to qualify for the professional diploma in marketing and thereby obtain graduate membership of that professional body.

Some full-time students may enrol on a master's or higher degree or postgraduate diploma programme but there are normally no mandatory grants available. Students are also required to obtain at least a first-class or upper second-class honours degree in order to be accepted for a higher degree. Many postgraduate programmes are also post-experience courses requiring the student to have worked for a few years before acceptance. In such cases, depending on experience, a lower second- or even third-class honours degree (or equivalent) may be accepted. Postgraduate courses for these awards can be found at universities, polytechnics and higher education colleges — the latter qualifications being validated in the main by the CNAA. Some of these courses are available on a part-time basis. A diagram showing the relationship of these various courses is shown in Figure 2.1.

Those unable or unwilling to pursue full-time further education courses, can enrol on a number of part-time programmes available at many centres throughout the country. Part-time (evenings) vocational education courses have their origins with the professional bodies, such as the Institute of Marketing (founded in 1911), which examined its first students in 1928. This, in fact, typified the way in which people became professionally qualified in their chosen career during the first half of this century and, to a large extent, still does to this day. The professional bodies' courses still account for approximately one third of all students enrolled on advanced business studies courses studying at further and higher educational colleges in the UK (DES Report INS56/12/0178–183/86–N518/85). It is no surprise, therefore, to learn that many students, both in the UK and throughout the world, still value highly the appropriate professional body's diploma and their membership of the professional institute.

With the relative cut-back in educational resource provision in the UK, the number of places available for both full-time and part-time students is limited and it may be necessary for you to take a course of instruction via a correspondence college or some other distance-learning programme — again, full details are obtainable from the professional body or, for example, by writing direct to providers such as the Open University (Open Business School), specialized colleges or the leading correspondence schools.

Opportunities exist for appropriate marketing qualifications to be obtained via part-time study at all levels, depending on the stage at which you left full-time education. In a world which is becoming more competitive, it is not surprising that more and more employers are asking for higher level qualifications, as well as

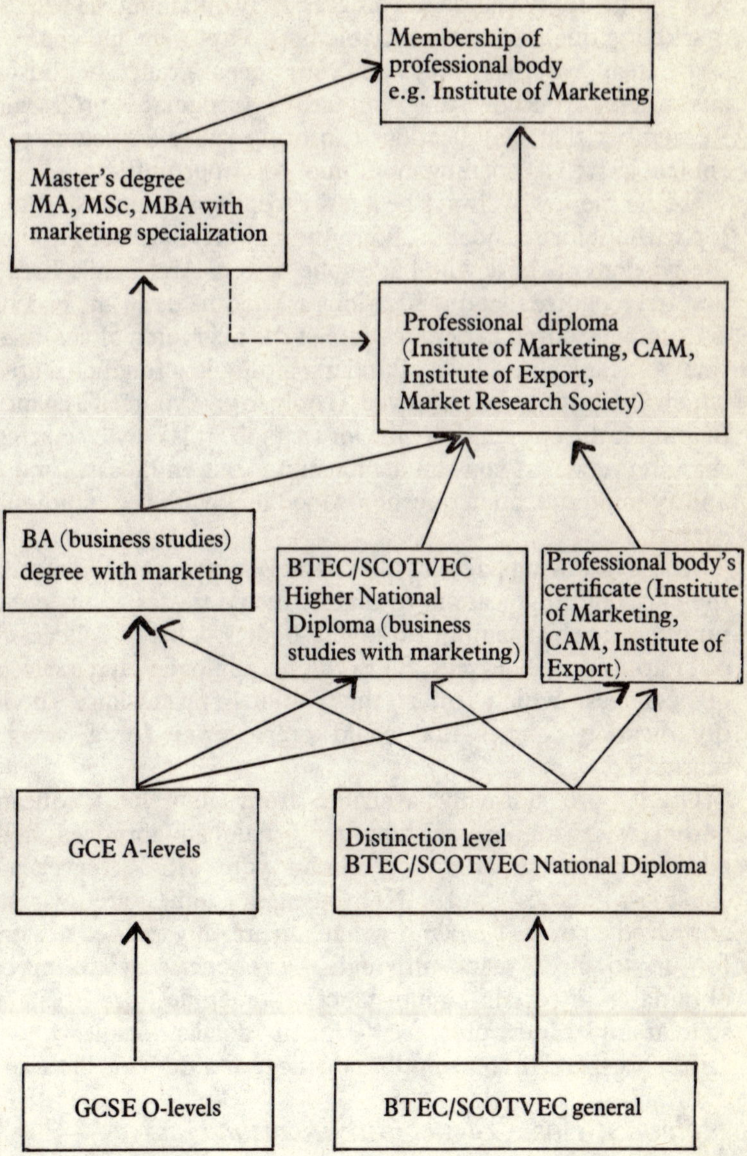

Figure 2.1 Qualifications for a career in marketing

experience, and, if you truly want to make marketing your career, you should apply yourself to progressively obtaining the necessary marketing qualifications to enable both employers and your work associates, whether they be your peer group or business customers, to know that you are a recognized professional. Remember that qualifications can bring you the freedom of job choice, as well as opening up promotion opportunities.

While there will always be a few exceptions who make it to the top without formal qualifications, the majority of us need to absorb the wisdom of those who have gone before. And, while I am the first to recognize that qualifications are not the be all and end all, it is usually essential to demonstrate at the beginning of your career that you can show a level of understanding in a functional area in which you hope to be employed, if only to give yourself a chance to be put on the chosen short-list for that job. It is only by getting to the interview that you can demonstrate your enthusiasm and real ability to do the job in question. Good luck with your studies and career.

In the following pages of this chapter, I have included details of the types of qualifications available, the addresses and telephone numbers of the main award-giving bodies, a list of colleges that offer appropriate degrees, BTEC higher diplomas, and a selection of colleges which offer the various professional bodies' qualification courses that could prepare you for a career in marketing.

Grants are normally available from your local education authority if you are wishing to pursue an approved higher education course after you obtain your GCE A-levels. BA (business studies) and HND business studies are two such approved courses. Remember that you are only entitled to a grant for up to three years, although discretionary awards may be obtainable in certain circumstances. Sometimes local trusts and scholarships can be obtained — for full details consult with your LEA, prospective course tutor or college and the local librarian.

Relevant Post O-level Qualification Courses — Full-time

Schools' Sixth Form and YTS Centre (selected) Certificates
Foundation Certificate in Marketing (Institute of Marketing

validated) — restricted availability till 1988. Entry qualifications: GCSE O-levels. Details from the Institute of Marketing.

Colleges of Further Education (Non-advanced Courses) Diplomas
BTEC National Diploma (Business Studies) or SCOTVEC National awards equivalent — widely available. Entry qualifications: GSCE O-level standard (four O-level subjects).

Colleges of FE and Higher Education (including Polytechnics') Diplomas
BTEC Higher National Diploma (Business Studies) or SCOTVEC Higher National awards equivalent — widely available. Entry qualifications: GCE A-level (minimum four O-level subjects, with one GCE A-level) or BTEC National Award.

Polytechnic and Colleges of Higher Education First Degrees
CNAA degrees in business studies with marketing specialization — sandwich course one year in industry — widely available at polytechnics and colleges of higher education. Entry qualifications: minimum of two good GCE A-levels (minimum of five GCE subjects, two of which must be at A-level).

Also available are more specialist degrees such as: BA (marketing and engineering) and BA (marketing and textiles) available at Huddersfield Polytechnic.

University First Degrees in Marketing
- Strathclyde University, BA(hons) marketing — four years. Also, BA joint honours courses with marketing and economics, and accountancy
- Lancaster University, BSc management sciences (marketing)
- Newcastle University, BSc agricultural marketing
- Aberystwyth, BSc agriculture and food marketing
- Reading University, BSc food science, food economics and marketing
- Salford University, BA modern languages and marketing studies

University Higher Degrees in Marketing from Business Schools, Universities, Polytechnics and Colleges of Higher Education

- Aberystwyth University, MSc agricultural and food marketing
- Bradford University, MPhil/PhD
- City University (London), MBA/PhD, MBA marketing
- Humberside College of HE, MBA, three years part-time
- Lancaster University, MPhil/PhD, MA, MSc Marketing
- Manchester University, MBA advanced marketing management or research for marketing decisions, one year
- Newcastle University, MSc/PhD, MSc marketing, one year
- Salford University, MA or MSc marketing and a foreign language
- Sheffield City Polytechnic, MSc management studies, four years part-time
- Strathclyde University, MSc/PhD, MSc marketing, one year
- Surrey University, MSc marketing for overseas students), two years
- Ulster University, MSc product development
- University of Manchester Institute of Science and Technology (UMIST), MSc marketing, one year
- Thames Polytechnic, MA in management studies, part-time

Postgraduate Diplomas in Marketing (CNAA or College Validated)

- The Polytechnic of Central London, diploma in marketing, one year
- Kingston Polytechnic, diploma in marketing, one year; diploma in direct marketing
- Bristol Polytechnic, postgraduate diploma in marketing
- Liverpool Polytechnic, diploma in marketing management, one year
- Manchester University/UMIST, diploma in marketing, one year
- Newcastle University, diploma in agricultural marketing
- North East London Polytechnic, diploma in marketing
- North Staffs Polytechnic, diploma in international marketing, one year
- Sheffield City Polytechnic, diploma in marketing, one year
- Strathclyde University, diploma in marketing, one year
- Ulster Polytechnic, diploma in marketing, two years part-time

- Newcastle upon Tyne Polytechnic, diploma in marketing, one year
- Polytechnic of Wales, diploma in marketing, one year; diploma in analytical marketing

- It should be noted that this is not an exhaustive list and new courses are being developed all the time. You should, therefore, always check with other preferred colleges to see what other programmes of study are being offered.

In respect of CNAA degrees, a directory of courses can be obtained by writing directly to the Council for National Academic Awards, 344–354 Gray's Inn Road, London WC1X 8BP.

Relevant Qualification Courses — Part-Time

Some BTEC/SCOTVEC higher awards are available on a part-time basis and so are a number of CNAA bachelor degrees — further information on these courses can be obtained by writing directly to BTEC, Berkshire House, 168–173 High Holborn, London WC1C 7AG, SCOTVEC, 22 Great King Street, Edinburgh EH3 6QH; 031 557 4555 or CNAA, 344–354, Gray's Inn Road, London WC1X 8BP.

Professional Courses

Professional courses are, however, almost entirely offered on a part-time basis with the evenings-only mode the most common. The Institute of Marketing's certificate in sales management, certificate in marketing and diploma in marketing can normally be found at the following colleges. (The CAM and Institute of Export courses are available at some of the colleges listed.)

County, College and Telephone Number	*Institute of Marketing* Certificate	*Institute of Marketing* Diploma
Avon		
Bristol Polytechnic 0272 656261		✓
Filton Technical College 0272 694217	✓	

Name and telephone number	*Institute of Marketing* Certificate	Diploma
Beds		
Luton College of Higher Education 0582 34111		✓
Berks		
Slough College of Higher Education 0753 34585	✓	✓
Bucks		
Bucks College of Higher Education 0494 38266	✓	✓
Cambs		
Cambridge College of Further Education 0223 357545	✓	
Peterborough Regional College 0733 67366	✓	✓
Cheshire		
Halton College 051–423 1391	✓	
Cleveland		
Stockton — Billingham Technical College 0642 552101	✓	
Derbyshire		
Chesterfield College of Technology & Arts 0246 31212	✓	
Devon		
East Devon College of Further Education 0884 254247	✓	✓
Plymouth College of Further Education 0752 264746	✓	

Name and telephone number	*Institute of Marketing* Certificate	Diploma
Dorset		
Dorset Institute of Higher Education 0202 524111	✓	✓
Durham		
New College (Durham) 0385 62421	✓	
Essex		
Barking College of Technology 01 599 3977	✓	
Colchester Institute of Higher Education 0255 422324		✓
Havering Technical College 04024 422324	✓	
Thurrock Technical College 07088 63011		✓
Glos		
GLOSCAT 0452 426821/426813	✓	✓
Hants		
Basingstoke Technical College 0256 471771		✓
Farnborough Technical College 0252 313772	✓	✓
Southampton College of Higher Education 0703 229381		✓
Herts		
Watford College 0923 41211	✓	✓

Name and telephone number	*Institute of Marketing* *Certificate*	*Diploma*
Humberside		
Humberside College of Higher Education 0482 41451		✓
Hull College of Further Education 0482 29943	✓	
Lancs		
Blackburn College 0254 55144	✓	✓
Wigan College of Technology 0257 421537	✓	✓
Charles Keene College of Further Education 0533 56037	✓	
Leics		
Leicester Polytechnic 0533 551551		✓
Wigston College of Further Education 0533 885051	✓	
London area		
City of London Polytechnic 01–283 1030	✓	✓
College for the Distributive Trades 01–839 1547	✓	✓
Croydon College 01–688 5700	✓	✓
Ealing College of Higher Education 01–579 4111		✓
Hammersmith & West London College 01–741 1688		✓

Name and telephone number	*Institute of Marketing* Certificate	Diploma
Harrow College of Art & Technology 01–864 5422	✓	✓
Middlesex Polytechnic 01–202 6545		✓
Polytechnic of the South Bank 01–928 8989		✓
Greater Manchester		
Manchester Polytechnic 061–228 6171		✓
Salford College of Technology 061–736 6541	✓	✓
St. Johns College of Further Education 061–831 7091	✓	
Stockport Technical College 061–480 7331	✓	✓
Norfolk		
Norwich City College of Further & Higher Education 0603 660011	✓	
Northants		
Nene College 0604 715000	✓	✓
Northumberland Technical College 0670 813248	✓	
Notts		
Trent Polytechnic 0602 418248	✓	✓

Name and telephone number	*Institute of Marketing Certificate*	*Diploma*
South Nottinghamshire College of Further Education 0602 812125	✓	
Staffs		
Burton on Trent Technical College 0283 45401	✓	
North Staffordshire Polytechnic 0782 412515		✓
Surrey		
Brooklands Technical College 0932 53300	✓	
Sussex		
Crawley College of Technology 0293 25686	✓	
Tyne & Wear		
Newcastle Polytechnic 0632 326002		✓
Warwicks		
East Warwickshire College of Further Education 0788 73133	✓	✓
Sutton Coldfield College of Further Education 021–355 5671	✓	✓
West Midlands		
City of Birmingham Polytechnic 021–356 6911		✓
Tile Hill College 0203 461444	✓	

Name and telephone number	*Institute of Marketing* *Certificate*	*Diploma*
Sandwell College 021–569 4615	✓	✓
Wolverhampton Polytechnic 0902 28286		✓
Wilts		
Swindon College 0793 40131	✓	
Trowbridge Techincal College 02214 66241	✓	✓
Worcs		
*Redditch College of Further Education 0527 63607	✓	✓
*Feasibility scheme available		
Yorkshire		
Keighley Technical College 0535 665421	✓	
Leeds Polytechnic 0532 439726		✓
Park Lane College of Further Education 0532 434380	✓	
Scarborough Technical College 0723 372105	✓	
Richmond College of Further Education 0742 392621	✓	
Sheffield City Polytechnic 0742 20911		✓

Name and telephone number	*Institute of Marketing* Certificate	*Institute of Marketing* Diploma
Trinity and All Saints College 0532 584341	✓	
York College of Art and Technology 0904 704141	✓	
Northern Ireland		
Belfast College of Technology 0232 27244	✓	✓
Newry Technical College 0693 61071	✓	
North Down College of Further Education 0274 462254	✓	
Ulster University 0231 65131		✓
Eire		
Carlow Regional Techincal College 0503 31324	✓	
Scotland		
Glasgow Scarborough Technical College and Distribution 041–552 3941	✓	✓
Kirkaldy Technical College 0592 268591	✓	✓
Napier College of Commerce & Technology 031–447 7070		✓
Robert Gordon's Institute of Technology 0224 482211		✓

	Institute of Marketing	
Name and telephone number	*Certificate*	*Diploma*
Wales		
Gwent College of Higher Education 0633 51525		✓
North East Wales Institute of Higher Education 0244 817531	✓	
Rumney College of Technology 0222 465475	✓	
Correspondence Colleges		
International Correspondence School (ICS) 041–221 2926	✓	✓
Metropolitan College/Wolsey Hall 0865 52200	✓	✓
Pitman's Correspondence College 01–947 6993		
Rapid Results College 01–947 7272	✓	✓

*This is not an exhaustive list and more up-to-date information can be obtained by writing directly to the professional body concerned.

In addition to the above, the British Direct Marketing Association's Diploma can be obtained from Kingston or Bristol Polytechnic. Further information is available from the polytechnics concerned.

Private Colleges

For overseas students and those who may wish to take a full-time course, a number of private colleges have been approved as centres for tuition. An up-to-date list of the approved private colleges can be obtained from the professional bodies concerned.

Names and Addresses of Award-Giving Bodies

BTEC,
Berkshire House,
168–173 High Holborn,
London WC1V 7AG.
01–379 7088

or

Central House,
Upper Woburn Place,
London WC1H 0HH.
01–388 3288

SCOTVEC
22 Great King Street
Edinburgh EH3 6QH
031–557 4555

or

38 Queen Street
Glasgow
G1 3DY
041–248 7900

CNAA,
344–354 Gray's Inn Road,
London WC1X 8BP.
01–278 4411

Institute of Marketing,
Moor Hall,
Cookham,
Berks SL6 9QH
06285 24922

The CAM Foundation,
Abford House,
15 Wilton Road,
London SW1V 1NJ.
01–828 7506/2777

The Market Research Society,
175 Oxford Street
London W1R 1TA.
01–439 2585

The Institute of Export,
64 Clifton Street,
London EC2.
01–247 9812

Open University,
Open Business School,
Walton Hall,
Milton Keynes MK7 6AA.
0908 74066

3. Personality and Your Career

Patricia Mann

The diversity of career opportunities in public relations, advertising and marketing might be expected to accommodate an equally wide range of personalities and talents. In practice, there are certain attributes which are common to virtually all of them; characteristics which are universally desirable.

One key attribute is the ability to work as a member of a team. These are not careers for those who work best in isolation, though the salesman is perhaps in a special category here. Within an advertising agency, for example, each function of the account group — marketing, media, creative, administrative — is interrelated and interdependent. The marketing function in industry interacts with every aspect of manufacturing and selling, from product design to distribution. Public relations requires liaison between the various departments of an organization and its many publics. Any of these working environments demands self-reliance and a degree of independence, but has no place for the self-important prima donna. So anyone who is a loner, or who always has to be right, or who is bossily competitive, or has no sense of compromise, or is inflexibly self-opinionated, is unlikely to be either happy or successful. Nor will the people he or she is expected to work with find the relationship productive.

A natural extension of team work is the ability to communicate clearly, orally and in writing. A muddled brief not only diverts expensive resources up blind alleys; it creates unnecessary frustration amongst those trying to meet it. Ambiguous interpretation of market research findings could misdirect very expensive new product development plans. At worst, sloppy communication can elicit the exact opposite of the intended response. Clear communication involves an understanding of the audience to whom it is addressed — whether an individual colleague or a section of the public — and what they need to know. If you find it difficult to explain your ideas or your attitudes, or if you cannot easily see another person's point of view, think twice about a career in advertising and marketing. Practice does help, but a basic respect for words and their precise meaning and a facility for clear expression are not easily acquired.

A third attribute which is universally applicable is self-discipline, coupled with self-criticism and accuracy. New recruits to an advertising agency are often surprised by its disciplines, particularly as the environment tends to be lively and informal. The limits imposed by the advertising strategy require a well-developed critical faculty to recognize and reject good ideas that are inappropriate or misdirected and to select those that are worth developing. Beyond these constraints, there are the limitations of about seventy statutes and statutory instruments and a very stringently applied Code of Advertising Practice which place further limitation on the content and presentation of advertisements. Advertising is not for those who think rules are to be broken. Nor is it for the careless. Everyone in an advertising or marketing company has a need to check and re-check their own accuracy. A mistake by a copywriter or art director, if unchecked, might lead to a prosecution under the Trade Descriptions Act. A mistake by a media buyer could cost thousands of pounds. A mistake in a telephone number could invalidate an advertising campaign, by misdirecting consumers' attempts to get further information.

The general qualities required, therefore, can be summed up as the ability to work as part of a team, to communicate clearly, and to be accurate, self-critical and self-disciplined. If you have all these qualities, you are likely to have a substantial degree of self-confidence — and you will need it.

The following sections touch briefly on some of the specific attributes required for specific jobs.

Account Management

Within an advertising agency, account executives and account directors are the key administrators. They liaise between the client and agency, and between all the advertising agency's many services and the client, and need a sound understanding of how both sides work.

An account executive is expected to have an alarming range of qualities. Intelligence, decisiveness and the ability to communicate clearly and persuasively are basic. He or she must also be able to motivate people in order to bring together the different skills within the agency, and direct and co-ordinate their efforts. Tact, diplomacy and sympathy for another person's viewpoint are important and mental flexibility is also necessary, to keep a number of simultaneous activities under control and to stay calm under pressure. Account executives have to earn the trust and confidence of all the people with whom they work and be sensitive enough to know when to cajole, bully, encourage, support or sympathize. And they have to be modest enough to disguise such a catalogue of virtues.

There are of course many variants and levels within "Account Management", and many of the specialist fields of communication carry different titles, and indeed require different qualities (e.g. the role of an "Account Administrator" in Recruitment Advertising). The basic qualities for the function of representing Client to Agency and vice versa are, however, common throughout.

Creative

Copywriters and artists both need an inexhaustible fund of ideas, an infinite capacity for expressing them in different ways and the self-critical faculty to reject those that are inappropriate. Advertising is not for fine artists manqués, nor for writers who want to pay the rent while working on a novel. It is for those who enjoy the challenge and stimulus of working within the disciplines of a narrow brief, the confines of limited space or airtime, and the restrictions of both laws and a strictly applied code of practice. Directness and brevity of expression are at a premium, and so is versatility — to adapt to a variety of accounts and a variety of problems where communication skills may be applied.

Considerable resilience is also required, to go on being involved, enthusiastic, innovative and original when ideas have to be discarded or altered. Self-criticism is probably more important to creative people than to any others in the agency. Their ideas must be relevant to the problem. The style must be a function of the product or service to be advertised, not a hallmark of the copywriter's or artist's individuality. Wit and humour have their place, but the distinction has to be drawn between relevance and self-indulgence.

Marketing

The processes of product marketing have been defined as "the art, science and practice of bringing the right goods and services to the consumer in the most efficient and profitable way". It is possible to be precise and scientific about many aspects of marketing, but it also requires flair and sensitivity. The brand manager is, as it were, managing director of a division of the company — the brand or group of brands for which he or she is responsible. It has been said that his bitterest competitors are his colleagues, the "managing directors" of other brands made by the company. Each of them is concerned to get more than a fair share of Research and Development expertise, salesmen's time and all the other company activities that create and maintain successful brands.

The brand manager has considerable responsibility and influence but comparatively little direct power. In order to get things done, to make things happen, an organized, action-orientated, disciplined and money-conscious person is needed. But that alone is not enough. He or she must also be sensitive to the consumer's changing needs and attitudes, inventive and perceptive.

The majority of brand management opportunities are given to graduates. Many companies suggest that the particular discipline is relatively unimportant. The Chairman of one large company has a different view. "I am clear — whether I am recruiting in this country, or in continental Europe, or in North America — that I am primarily interested in graduates who have had logic-based training. I like mathematicians, physicists, classicists, lawyers: people who have had to think about differences of meaning, who have been required to be very precise in their choice of words, who are able to think of the essence of a problem in precise terms. I also look for people who are honest and morally courageous, which is harder to identify than other characteristics when recruiting. We have to look facts fairly and squarely in the face, including recognizing when a product is just not good enough, recognizing when advertising is not earning more than its cost, recognizing when a competitor has the edge on us."

Market Research

Market research is a means of acquiring knowledge upon which business decisions may be based by analysing existing facts or finding out new information. Familiarity with figures is a basic requirement although it is not essential to be a mathematician or statistician. Even more important is objectivity. It would be very easy for personal beliefs or feelings to influence the findings of research, and it is important that such personal bias is eliminated. The essential qualities for research interviewers are honesty, tact, courtesy, accuracy and reliability. They must also be observant, as information may be qualified by the way in which it is given. Nevertheless, the interviewer's own opinions or interpretation should neither influence the person being interviewed nor colour the factual reporting of the interviewee's responses. Those with strong, personal opinions which they find it difficult to conceal are unlikely to make useful interviewers.

Research executives are responsible for helping to define the problem, suggesting the best means of finding the information upon which decisions may be based, and presenting the findings. Clear, unambiguous expression is extremely important. He or she also needs a sympathy with figures, an orderly and methodical approach, and objectivity. A talent for recognizing useful and usable information and relating it to problems tends to come with practice, rather than as an innate characteristic.

Media

The variety of career opportunities with media make it difficult to generalize. Those employed by the media to sell the advertisement space they carry are likely to be confident and extrovert. Media planners, who are responsible for the allocation of appropriations, may be more introspective. Media buyers are required to negotiate the best airtime and space and must be tough enough to say "no" when necessary. All of these very different jobs have in common the need for accuracy and scrupulous attention to detail. Even when computers handle much of the routine, the work must be carefully checked. A talent for figures is extremely important for all media work as well as a degree of creative judgement, to evaluate not only the audiences reached through each medium but also the environment in which its advertisements appear.

Public Relations

Public relations is concerned with planned communications to promote goodwill and mutual understanding between an organization and its many "publics". These "publics" may include customers, potential customers, former customers, the general public, employees, trade unions, shareholders, the Government, local communities, town planning authorities, shopkeepers, consumer groups, environmentalists and a whole host of other interests. A sound knowledge of communications can be acquired, but a genuine interest in other people's beliefs, attitudes and behaviour and the ability to see someone else's point of view is a basic requirement. Organizing ability, a pleasant personality and enough adaptability to talk to people with widely disparate backgrounds and interests are important, as is the ability to communicate fluently, accurately and objectively in speech and writing.

How Competitive Are You?

No one would pretend that jobs in communication, advertising and marketing are easily obtained. Openings are limited and the competition for jobs is plentiful. In some ways, this is an advantage. You will need to be determined, persistent and resilient, you will need to demonstrate that you can communicate, you will need to be self-critical and self-disciplined in order to find your first job. And all these qualities will be essential to you if you are to make a successful career in one of these fields. If you enjoy identifying the opportunities and working out the appropriate approach, and thrive on the competition, then you are likely to find your feet on the first step. And if you don't, perhaps you would be happier doing something else anyway.

4. Marketing

Michael J. Baker

Introduction

It is generally accepted that two of the most significant factors contributing to economic growth and the standard of living are "task specialization" and the "division of labour". The principle involved is simple and obvious — if we concentrate our energies on producing those goods or services we are best at producing, and organize the production act to minimize the time lost through changing from one task to another (ultimately by breaking the job down into a series of discrete acts each performed by a different individual) then we will maximize our collective production efficiency. However, the creation of supply in and of itself is a sterile act, for goods and services only possess value to the extent that they are desired and consumed. The output of the most sophisticated factory in the world is useless unless there are people with a need for that output who can obtain supplies of it. Clearly we need some mechanism for ensuring that those with a need for products are put in contact with those with a supply of that product and this mechanism is the *market*.

In turn, the process involved in equating supply and demand may be characterized as *exchange* while the primary business function responsible for organizing such exchange is *marketing*.

The Marketing Concept

Perhaps the most important single statement which can be made about the marketing concept is that it is a state of mind which recognizes that demand should be a primary determinant of supply. Not the primary determinant, for there are many other considerations which may assume precedence. For example an organization has responsibilities to its shareholders and its employees and in the short to medium term it might be highly irresponsible to respond directly to changes in consumer preferences. It is for this reason that firms try to plan change and phase it so that it does not make past investment obsolete prematurely nor render personnel redundant when they might be retrained or redeployed.

In the long run, however, it is clear that the interests of the firm will be best served to the extent that it can anticipate changing consumer needs and organize its resources to meet these needs. It is in trying to anticipate changing consumer needs that management is required to adopt a very different approach from that associated with the more traditional finance and production functions, each of which tends to have a rather different orientation.

The Marketing Mix

The marketing mix is a phrase devised by Professor Neil Borden of the Harvard Business School to distinguish the range of "ingredients" which may be found in a marketing programme as well as the process whereby they may be combined according to a variety of recipes in order to meet different needs. According to Borden the elements of the mix fall into twelve categories as follows:

1 *Product planning* Policies and procedures relating to
  (a) product lines to be offered — qualities, design, etc.
  (b) the markets to sell — whom, where, when, and in what quantity
  (c) new product policy — research and development programme.

2 *Pricing* Policies and procedures relating to
  (a) the level of prices to adopt
  (b) the specific prices to adopt (odd—even, etc.)
  (c) price policy — one price or varying price, price maintenance, use of list prices, etc.
  (d) the margins to adopt — for company, for the trade.

3 *Branding* Policies and procedures relating to
(a) selection of trade marks
(b) brand policy — individualized or family brand
(c) sale under private brand or unbranded.

4 *Channels of Distribution* Policies and procedures relating to
(a) the channels to use between plant and consumer
(b) the degree of selectivity among wholesalers and retailers
(c) efforts to gain the co-operation of the trade.

5 *Personal Selling* Policies and procedures relating to the burden to be placed on personal selling and the methods to be employed in
(a) the manufacturer's organization
(b) the wholesale segment of the trade
(c) the retail segment of the trade.

6 *Advertising* Policies and procedures relating to
(a) the amount to spend — i.e. the burden to be placed on advertising
(b) the copy platform to adopt (i) product image desired, (ii) corporate image desired
(c) the mix of advertising — to the trade, through the trade — to consumers.

7 *Promotion* Policies and procedures relating to
(a) the burden to place on special selling plans or devices directed at or through the trade
(b) the form of these devices for consumer promotions, for trade promotions.

8 *Packaging* Policies and procedures relating to formulation of package and label.

9 *Display* Policies and procedures relating to
(a) the burden to be put on display to help effect sales
(b) the methods to adopt to secure display.

10 *Servicing* Policies and procedures relating to providing service needed.

11 *Physical Handling* Policies and procedures relating to
(a) warehousing
(b) transportation
(c) inventories.

12 *Fact Finding and Analysis* Policies and procedures relating to the securing, analysis, and use of facts in marketing operations.

Although Borden claims that this list is only his own and that others may wish to develop their own alternatives, few if any have challenged it as a comprehensive statement of the main, discrete areas of marketing activity. However most would agree that the twelfth area, "Fact Finding and Analysis", might be placed more logically at the beginning rather than at the end of the list, for it is on this that the remainder depend for guidance and direction. Also the function is more usually referred to as *marketing research* and enjoys a clear and separate identity as we shall see when reviewing some of the more common career opportunities prior to the detailed examination contained in the remainder of the book. A pictorial representation of the major elements is contained in Figure 4.1.

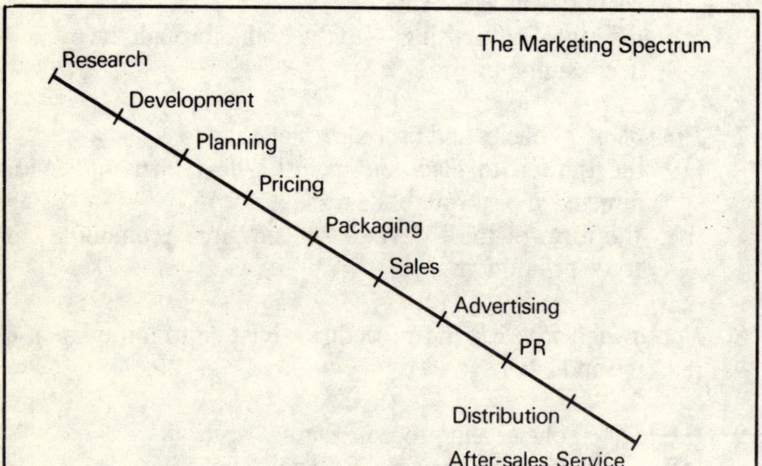

Figure 4.1 The Marketing Spectrum
(*Reproduced by permission of the Institute of Marketing*)

We have already suggested that different combinations of ingredients (or different quantities of individual ingredients) will lead to distinctive recipes for action under different circumstances. A major responsibility of the marketing function is to assess different sets of circumstances and propose the most appropriate mix to meet the situation. In doing so Borden postulates four main sets of factors which will influence management's choice:

1 *Consumers' Buying Behaviour* as determined by
   (a) their motivation in purchasing
   (b) their buying habits
   (c) their living habits
   (d) their environment (present and future as revealed by trends, for environment influences consumers' attitudes toward products and their use of them)
   (e) their number (i.e., how many)
   (f) their buying power.

2 *The Trade's Behaviour* Wholesalers' and retailers' behaviour, as influenced by
   (a) their motivations
   (b) their structure, practice and attitudes
   (c) trends in structure and procedures that portend change.

3 *Competitors' Position and Behaviour* as influenced by
   (a) industry and structure and the firms' relation thereto (i) size and strength of competitors, (ii) number of competitors and degree of industry concentration, and (iii) indirect competition — i.e., competition from other products
   (b) relation of supply to demand — oversupply or undersupply
   (c) product choices offered consumers by the industry: (i) in quality, (ii) in price, and (iii) in service
   (d) degree to which competitors compete on price versus non-price bases
   (e) competitors' motivations and attitudes — their likely response to the actions of other firms

(f) trends technological and social, portending change in supply and demand.

4 *Governmental Behaviour — Controls over Marketing*
(a) regulations over products
(b) regulations over pricing
(c) regulations over competitive practices
(d) regulations over advertising and promotional methods.

Discussion of the relative importance of these factors in different industries to firms of different size and structure is beyond the scope of this book. However, having identified a wide variety of marketing functions it will be helpful in this chapter to review some of these briefly as an introduction to later chapters which deal with them in greater depth. Specially we will look at Market Research, Product Management, Selling and Sales Management, Advertising and Promotion, Public Relations, Distribution, Marketing Management and International Marketing.

Marketing Research

The main objective of Marketing Research has been defined as "reducing the uncertainty surrounding business decisions", an objective which it achieves through the collection and analysis of data relevant to marketing problems. In every sense of the word marketing research is the intelligence function of marketing activity.

In common with other aspects of marketing, marketing research draws upon a diversity of disciplines and techniques and encompasses both qualitative and behavioural approaches to the assessments of opinions and attitudes as well as precise quantitative measurement of demand, usage, readership of print media, viewing habits, etc., etc. While the professional market researcher would be expected to have a sound knowledge of both the behavioural sciences and quantitative methods it is usual to find most practitioners gravitating towards one or the other by inclination and preference.

Following its emergence as a significant function in its own right in the 1930s, the distinction between qualitative and quantitative approaches was paralleled by a similar discrimination between research for consumer marketing decisions by contrast with industrial marketing problems, reaching its zenith in the 1950s with the fashion for motivational research. Unfortunately some of the excesses of the latter tended to bring the whole behavioural methodology into disrepute but this has now been overcome, resulting in a more judicious combination of qualitative and quantitative methods. Indeed with the advent of the computer we have seen the development of a number of powerful models and techniques which attempt to synthesize both types of data, e.g. perceptual mapping, multidimensional scaling.

From the foregoing it should be clear that some facility with numbers is a decided advantage for the prospective market researcher. However, this is equally true of most branches of marketing, and indeed business as a whole, and would-be entrants to the profession should not be put off if theirs is only a modest ability, for the primary need is for analytical skill in interpreting patterns in data rather than a high degree of mathematical skill as such.

It is probably true to say that market research is the most professional of all marketing activities, and it is widely accepted that UK researchers are in the forefront of developments in the field. The Market Research Society has a strong educational interest and awards a Diploma to persons achieving a satisfactory standard in its exams, or in the approved examinations of certain universities and polytechnics at the degree or post-graduate level.

Career prospects are good and an increasing number of organizations are setting up their own in-house market research function as well as making use of the many specialized agencies which offer their services on a contract basis or through the publication of regular reports such as the Neilson Retail Audit.

Product Management

Within the marketing profession there is a continuing debate about the most effective organizational structure, with much of the most animated discussion centering upon the middle-management activity described as product or brand management.

Brand management is generally believed to have been "invented" by General Electric who appointed a Product Manager in 1894 while Procter & Gamble appointed a Brand Manager to look after the marketing of Lava soap as long ago as 1928. In essence the idea of appointing a product or brand manager is to ensure that a designated individual will be responsible for integrating all the activities necessary to ensure the successful sale of that product, particularly where the company is producing a wide range of different products competing for the same end-use markets e.g. soap, detergents, confectionery lines, etc. More specifically the product manager will usually be responsible for liaising with the production function to ensure that adequate supplies of the product will be available in the packs, sizes and specification called for in the marketing plan, that advertising, sales promotion, merchandizing and point-of-sale display activities are co-ordinated, that the sales force are briefed concerning the promotion plan and will give the product the necessary support, that physical distribution will ensure supplies are delivered in accordance with sales orders taken and that steps are taken to monitor consumer reaction to the product and its marketing.

However the logic of concentrating upon the product has been criticized as being at odds with the marketing concept, for the emphasis is upon what the company is doing rather than upon the consumer. Thus there is a school of thought which argues that the organizational structure should be based on consumer needs and emphasize markets and market managers rather than products and product managers. Under such a market structure a manager would co-ordinate all marketing efforts for his company in a given market irrespective of the number of brands involved, e.g. "the household cleaning products market".

As a very broad generalization, market managers are most appropriate where the firm possesses highly distinctive and differentiated products while the product manager concept is best suited where the company has several brands all competing for the same end-use market. In the latter situation the market orientation would be superimposed at a higher managerial level.

The main failing of both product and market management also constitutes its greater attraction for young people wishing to make a career in business — namely it carries a very heavy burden of responsibility but lacks the necessary authority to impose decisions on the other functional managers involved. Thus the product/market manager has to be both diplomat and leader —

both of which abilities are in great demand for senior executive appointments — and young people who do well as product managers frequently gain accelerated promotion to senior management.

Appointment is usually by promotion from clerical or sales positions for school leavers while many companies offer direct entry to graduates. The financial rewards are usually high and the job offers great opportunities to the ambitious and more extrovert personality.

Within this section some mention must be made of product development. This is sometimes a specialized function in its own right, in which case it is usually associated with the research and development function, while often it is an *ad hoc* activity with multidisciplinary groups drawn from the major functional areas. Either way it is unlikely that persons interested in mainstream marketing would go directly into a product development appointment.

Selling and Sales Management

Personal selling is perhaps the best known and most visible marketing activity. For many it provides the most obvious and direct entry to a career in marketing and some experience of personal selling is usually required for more senior marketing appointments.

The cost of keeping a salesman "on the road" has escalated in recent years and most firms are very conscious of this. As a result, personal selling tends to be confined to situations where direct interaction between buyer and seller has a marked influence upon orders and sales or where the salesman performs important secondary functions such as merchandizing. That said, a survey undertaken towards the end of 1984 clearly indicated that personal selling still represents the biggest single expenditure in the marketing budget.

In crude terms, salesmen fall into two categories — "order makers" and "order takers". Order makers are most often encountered in the industrial situation, where the complex nature of the product demands close evaluation by the buyer and detailed interaction with the seller to ensure the buyer's needs will be met. By contrast "order taking" is usually found in situations where there is strong advertising and promotional support which tends to "pull" the product through the distribution channel from manufacture to ultimate consumer. These conditions are encountered most frequently in the case of mass consumption goods and in these circumstances the salesman's role is frequently extended to incorporate assistance wth point-of-sale display, etc.

All salesmen need to enjoy meeting people, to be good talkers and even better listeners. They must also have a certain resilience of character and modest optimism for there has yet to be a salesman who will not be "turned down" sometimes. In many respects these personal qualities are more important than formal qualifications. This is not to decry specialist knowledge but it is often easier to train someone with the right sort of personality in the technical aspects of a product than it is to translate a technical specialist into an accomplished salesman. It follows that in certain highly technical areas the man or woman with the specialist knowledge such as a degree in metallurgy or engineering plus the right personality will be able to enjoy a considerable premium in technical selling, as will be readily apparent from the classified advertising in any quality newspaper.

Advertising and Promotion

While selling sometimes suffers — as described in Chapter 5 — from an entirely unjustified "seedy" image derived from generations of music-hall jokes about commercial travellers, advertising tends to suffer from an over-glamorous image which totally belies the sheer hard work and dedication involved in developing effective advertising and promotional campaigns. It is true that advertising has an enormous appetite for creative people but it must always be remembered that while most businessmen are loath to interfere with the creative process itself, they have no inhibitions about criticizing the results of a given advertising campaign. Performance is judged by results in the market place. Advertising also suffers from a great deal of uninformed criticism, much of which seems to flow from the entirely unjustified assumption that the critic is immune to the powerful effects of campaigns which separate the rest of us from our hard-earned income in exchange for unnecessary and unwanted goods. Such criticism tends to ignore the basic truth of the definition of marketing which points out that "marketing is selling goods that don't come back to people who do". Or, put another way, the long-term prosperity of the firm depends upon delivering the promised satisfaction, for otherwise there will be no repeat purchases and, in the long term, these are the only certain guarantee of a firm's survival.

Another myth about advertising is that it is a homogeneous occupation requiring only one personality type. In reality advertising has need of researchers to measure audience needs and the efficiency of different messages and media; it needs creative people to devise ways of communicating a message so that it will achieve its purpose in competition with hundreds of other competing messages; it needs production specialists to translate creative concepts into words and pictures for a variety of different media; it needs specialists to place the advertising in the most effective combination of available media to achieve the maximum impact at the lowest cost, and it needs executives to liaise with clients (or agencies) to ensure that business objectives are transformed into effective advertising/promotional campaigns.

Given the wide range of jobs in advertising there is room for all sorts of talents. School leavers may gain direct employment and work their way up the promotional ladder while those with specialist and/or graduate qualifications may aspire to direct appointment to a specific job in one of the areas outlined above.

Public Relations

While a great deal of advertising is handled by agencies servicing the needs of a diverse range of client companies it is probably true to say that more PR work is executed by the firm on its own behalf than through the use of specialist agencies. This distinction undoubtedly owes as much to the fact that public relations is a top management responsibility whereas most advertising is an operational responsibility delegated to the next tier of management as it does to the fact that media owners pay advertising agencies a commission on purchases but rarely give a discount to the direct purchaser, i.e., the advertiser will get better value for his money by using an agency.

The Institute of Marketing's pamphlet "A Qualification in Marketing" has this to say about Public Relations:

"Public Relations practice, in the comprehensive sense, is the deliberate planned and sustained effort to establish and maintain mutual understanding between an organization and its public. In industry and commerce there are two distinct areas of public relations practice: the consultancies and the public relations departments of companies. There are considerable opportunities for a progressive career in public relations in that part of its work which is related to marketing. Because public relations is a two-way exercise — keeping the public informed on company developments, and keeping the company management informed on public reactions to those developments — close contact with top management is essential, and this frequently leads to widened responsibilities and promotions within an organization. The public relations man's job is to build bridges of understanding and appreciation between the company and those with whom it wishes to maintain contact. To do this involves knowledge of the many ways of finding out what people think and want, and of the various means of communicating information and ideas to people. The principal media for organized public relations as a backing to marketing are the Press, films, radio, television, exhibitions, lectures, speeches, visual aids and printed material. The public relations executive must have a working knowledge of these media so that he can use them to the greatest effect. Among the many qualities needed for success in public relations work are sound judgement, a sense of social responsibility, a flair for discovering facts that need to be communicated, coupled with a skill in selecting and handling the best means of communicating them. On the personal side, the Public Relations Officer needs to cultivate an agile and imaginative mind, enthusiasm and enterprise, good taste, tolerance, tact and discretion".

Distribution

Distribution is the Cinderella of marketing — physical distribution and warehousing (or "logistics" as it is sometimes termed) is seen as dull,while retail distribution is often dismissed as a job which lacks challenge and also requires you to work weekends. As a result of these largely unfounded stereotypes there is a scarcity of well-qualified recruits into the area and a far greater opportunity for accelerated promotion than in other areas of marketing.

It was Peter Drucker who described distribution as "the dark continent of business" for until comparatively recently it has been largely ignored with the result that as an area it has the greatest unexploited potential for development. The combination of operational research techniques which offer optimum theoretical solutions to inventory and transportation problems coupled with computerized systems for handling and recording the movement and sale of goods, holds out great promise for significant operational savings in the final decades of the century. Article numbering, whereby electronic check-outs can prepare a bill of sale and adjust stock levels simultaneously, is already a reality and the possibility of "telemarketing" is no longer a figment of the science-fiction writer's imagination. Clearly physical distribution has much to offer the ambitious new entrant.

The same is true of retailing, where the traditional image of the corner shop is at odds with the enormous concentration in retail buying power which has occurred in recent years with the result that over seventy per cent of all retail purchases are controlled by less than 1,500 buying points. As a result of this concentration, retail organizations exercise enormous influence over the production and marketing systems and offer a challenging opportunity for any young person with sufficient independence of mind to appreciate their potential.

International Marketing

While international marketing is sometimes distinguished as a separate area, in reality the functional responsibilities are very similar to those met with in the domestic environment. However for people with a facility for languages and an interest in the culture and institutions of other countries, international marketing provides an added attraction. Formal language qualifications are a distinct advantage for entry into the international side of the marketing operation, although many firms will provide appropriate training for employees who have demonstrated competence in the home market and are anxious to transfer.

Marketing Management

There is no single or simple definition of marketing management and its scope and responsibility will vary enormously according to the size of the firm, the nature of the product it is selling, and the market it is selling into. In general, however, marketing management is responsible for co-ordinating the various elements of the marketing mix and proposing the most effective combination to meet particular marketing problems. Its responsibilities are such that experience in a specialist activity is an inevitable prerequisite for appointment, so that it should be regarded as a job to aspire to rather than one to which direct entry can be made.

A survey undertaken by Heidrick and Struggles in conjunction with the Institute of Marketing into the responsibilities, background, experience and remuneration of chief marketing executives in the United Kingdom clearly shows that the role of marketing has grown significantly in the past five years. Thus the survey found that: "the chief marketing executive has in the past five years steadily become more important as a strategic driving force within companies. This trend, attributed to the need for better corporate response to the market place in order to survive the recent years of recession, is seen across the board, from companies where the chief marketing executive is the first to have been appointed, through to the large marketing-led consumer goods companies. Consolidation of this trend is foreseen in the coming five years."

In addition to confirming the growing role which marketing is playing in the overall affairs of companies, the study confirms that: "The proportion of chief marketing executives who have a degree has increased in recent years; sixty-one per cent of respondents who have been in their current jobs for less than three years have degrees, compared with fifty-three per cent of those who have been in their jobs longer than this." The analysis also indicates quite clearly that in recent years there has been an increasing emphasis on the promotion of persons with formal qualifications in marketing.

For those contemplating a career in marketing management, a particularly encouraging trend has been that whereas the emphasis has shifted from the secondary or manufacturing industries to the tertiary or service sector, there has been no lessening in the importance attached to the marketing function. Indeed, there is considerable evidence to suggest that there is growing recognition of the relevance of marketing principles and practice to service and public sector organizations because all businesses and institutions ultimately rely on increasing revenue to fulfil their obligations and objectives. Both of these areas, therefore, now offer increasing opportunities for a rewarding career in marketing.

The message is clear. There is a growing demand for marketing personnel in all kinds of organization, and preference will be given to those with a recognized qualification in the subject.

Summary

In this chapter we have attempted to define the nature of marketing and distinguish between the concept and the function. We have argued that the concept is concerned with maximizing satisfaction by ensuring that consumer needs and preferences are a primary determinant of what shall be made available for consumption. We have also expressed the opinion that this viewpoint can, and indeed *should*, be held by all managers irrespective of their particular job function.

However, marketing is also an activity comprising a number of distinct elements which need to be combined in varying proportions in order to achieve different objectives. Collectively we refer to these elements as the marketing mix, and the remainder of the chapter has provided a thumbnail sketch of the major components of this mix. In the remainder of the book the career opportunities associated with the main mix elements will be discussed in greater detail.

5. Selling

Richard N. Skinner

If you are interested in marketing as a career, you should give serious thought to when and how you are going to gain experience in selling. At least it would seem logical to believe that selling, in the sense of direct, face-to-face contact with customers and their wants, has an essential part to play in the development of a fully effective marketing man or woman. And yet, if you were to ask any random group of students what they wanted to do when they left college, how many would say: "I want to be a salesman"? And indeed how many salesmen, even successful salesmen, could say truthfully that they deliberately chose selling as a career? However inevitable success, and hindsight, make it seem, they probably drifted into selling through a variety of channels and then found it suited them well.

This apparent paradox between the importance of selling experience and the haphazard routes by which it has in the past been gathered, springs from two causes. In the first place, there are many selling jobs which require a background of business experience, and are therefore not open to beginners. Secondly, and of much greater significance, there is a certain ambiguity of attitude on the part of society towards selling, which tends to make young people reluctant to see it as a professional activity on a par with the work of doctors, solicitors, social workers or engineers. We shall be looking at the first problem later in this chapter, as a matter of timing your entry into selling. But unless the second issue is faced here and now you will not be likely to be concerned with timing, or with entry at any time.

How do you see selling at this moment? Is it something of a "con job", persuading people to buy things they do not really need? Are salesmen simply smooth talkers, or back-slapping buttonholers with a gift of the gab? Or is the image one of a seedy fellow burdened with a case of samples, knocking disconsolately on doors that seldom open? All of these notions, however self-contradictory they may be, are present in the public mind. Consumer organizations and governments tend to view salesmen as somehow parasitic on the processes of production and distribution that would operate quite smoothly without them. The Consumer Credit Act, for example, seeks to control methods of selling for the good of the supposedly helpless buyer. Is this necessary, or is it merely one aspect of an attitude which is generally unfavourable to any business run independently of state control? More importantly, how should these opinions affect your own views of selling as a career?

Experienced businessmen tend to ignore unfavourable attitudes to selling, as far as they are able. They know that there are unscrupulous salesmen, and unsuccessful salesmen, just as there are unscrupulous or unsuccessful accountants, solicitors or politicians. They also believe with some reason that these are a minority and that the vast majority of salesmen are doing something useful which contributes to the wealth of the community. Younger people, confronted with differing opinions, will not, and should not, be prepared to take any of this on trust.

It is therefore worth looking at the selling job afresh, to see just what it is, and why it is. After which we shall examine the different forms selling can take, attempt a picture of a "typical" salesman's day, and take a look at the tools of his trade. We will then be in a position to view selling as a career in itself and as a step to other marketing functions, with some grasp of the real issues involved, and free from the prejudices to which we are all exposed.

Personal Selling in the Buying Process

Salesmen and women are employed in a wide variety of businesses and their jobs are sometimes labelled according to the product they sell. Thus there are insurance salesmen, "space" salesmen employed by newspapers and journals, salesmen in pharmaceuticals, food, clothing, components, raw materials or capital goods. The selling of services is becoming increasingly important, medical and financial services, for example, and technical "know-how" such as computer installation. And yet these different forms of activity have a great deal in common and, given detailed knowledge of the product, a good salesman in one field can and does transfer his selling skills successfully to another field. So the product itself is of little help in defining or classifying the selling role.

A more promising approach is to consider the outlets to which selling is directed. There are, for instance, retail salesmen working in shops, door-to-door salesmen, wholesalers' salesmen and manufacturers' salesmen. There are also speciality salesmen calling on the end users in commerce and industry or on public authorities. Sometimes these selling roles are treated hierarchically, assuming some sort of pyramid with shop assistants at the bottom and whatever type of selling you yourself are doing at the top. This again ignores the common factors in selling and belittles the skills that may be involved in other selling roles. Nevertheless, there are differences between the types of selling we have mentioned which merit further consideration for the light they may throw on selling as a career.

Another kind of distinction is sometimes made between "action" selling and "application" selling. This relates partly to the type of customer involved. Some selling can be achieved in a fairly short space of time because the product can be related simply and quickly to a customer's needs. Perhaps a demonstration to show its merits is all that is required. By contrast "application" selling may involve surveys, reports, recommendations and meetings before the product can be matched to the customer's requirement. A considerably longer selling cycle is involved. Again there is nothing scientific about this distinction, although it does appear that some salesmen are more suited to the faster pace and quicker returns of action selling, while others may enjoy the feeling that they are part of a team, working with the customer to find the best solution to a problem.

None of these attempts at classification is entirely satisfactory, largely because they are too parochial. Selling is only one part of a process that is otherwise calling buying. To understand the selling job it is necessary to look at both sides of this process and at the part the salesman plays in the communications link between a company and its customers. Customers rarely see themselves simply as passive "sellees". They view their activity as buying, not as being sold to. So a closer look at buying can form a good starting point for a deeper consideration of the selling function.

As buyers customers may have several different tasks to perform. These have been classified as:

1 The Straight Rebuy
2 The Modified Rebuy
3 The New Buy.

From the buyer's point of view every purchase made falls into one or other of these categories. A manufacturer buying raw materials, a retailer restocking his shelves, an office manager buying carbon paper are all performing the routine task of the straight rebuy. The product to be purchased is defined precisely. No changes are required. The only factors likely to worry the buyer, granted that quality is maintained, are delivery and price.

In a modified rebuy there are changes. Perhaps updated designs and processes demand a different specification for components or materials, or the office manager wishes to try other grades and types of carbon paper to see if better results or greater economy can be obtained. By definition we are here dealing with a change of product and its fitness for its intended purpose looms at least as large as price and delivery in the mind of the buyer making his decision.

The new buy is the most difficult situation the buyer faces. Let us suppose that a company decides to consider electronic word-processing as an alternative to conventional typing. Instantly the type of carbon paper in use becomes of negligible importance. The whole typing operation — its objectives, its results, its cost — has now to be considered. The options available are a great deal wider than in the case of a straight rebuy or modified rebuy, and, most important for us, there is a need for much more information about the possible alternatives.

It is in fact possible to look at all three "buyclasses" in terms of the information requirement in each case. A straight rebuy demands no new information, only reassurance that the product will continue to be available at the right time and at the right price, and that its quality will be unimpaired. A modified rebuy demands information about alternative products. A new buy may well call for information not just on how one product compares with another but on how each alternative will affect the running of an operation, its cost and, where appropriate, its profitability.

How do prospective customers obtain this information? Certainly from commercials, catalogues, samples, advertisements and the opinion of existing users. Nevertheless the more complex the task of choosing, the less likely it will be that the buyer relies entirely on written information which cannot answer all his questions, and the more he will need the services of a salesman. The salesman's job, from a buyer's point of view, is therefore to provide information on what his product is, what it can do and how it compares with the alternatives available. Sometimes he has also to discuss the economics of adopting the product and the savings or the operating improvements that could stem from its use.

Sometimes the advice and information a salesman has to offer is his only "product". Selling services, as opposed to material objects, provides a substantial number of career opportunities. Market research, insurance, advertising, advice on financial planning or company acquisitions are examples of intangible products of this type. Nevertheless the benefits they bring are real enough to those who need them, and they will fit quite easily into one or other of the buyclasses we have defined, usually as modified rebuys or new buys.

Naturally as the buying task becomes more complex so more people are likely to be involved. In industrial buying one purchasing officer is usually sufficient to handle the straight rebuy. The modified rebuy may involve other departments or technical experts. New buys on the scale of our word-processing example will involve several departments and certainly require the understanding and approval of top management. This means that the salesman in that type of situation has to be capable of dealing with all the different departmental interests and levels of management involved in the decision-making process.

From this it would appear that the salesman's role is vital to the development of industry and commerce. Buyers could not function without salesmen and the information and help they bring. If they did not exist, they would have to be invented. As a matter of interest, in places where they do not officially exist, for example in Eastern European countries, they are now being invented! The salesman is an important, often the most important, link in the communication chain on which industry depends. His role is highly responsible, since customers rely on and act upon his advice, and the consequences of a wrong decision based on bad advice can be serious.

Nevertheless there is another way of looking at the salesman's job, and that is from the point of view of the company employing him. He is not, after all, paid simply to give service and sound advice to his customers: he is paid to get orders. He may be used defensively, to keep existing customers satisfied, or aggressively, to add new customers or capture the accounts of competitors. In either case there is from the company's point of view only one justification for his activities and that is the level of business obtained. There are of course other ways of getting orders, apart from personal selling. Advertising, direct mail, calls from service men, the recommendations of users can all generate business. Most established companies would still have some sales, even if no salesmen at all were employed. The cost of adding direct selling to the overheads of a company has to be justified by the extra business it brings.

It is possible to compare, for each of the buying situations we have identified, the needs of the customer with the aims of the supplying company and to summarize the factors which will enable a salesman to succeed in meeting the demands of both parties. This may provide a framework into which individual selling jobs may be slotted, whatever the product and regardless of whether the customer is an individual, a company or a government body (Table 5.1). For the sake of clarity when dealing with rebuy situations it is convenient to distinguish the aims of the "in" supplier defending an existing business connection, from those of the "out" supplier attempting to break in.

No doubt this model could be refined further to display the salesman's role and the requirements of the job in greater detail but it does serve to illustrate the growing complexity of the selling task as we move from the straight rebuy towards the new buy situation. The part the salesman has to play in creating change and in making effective his company's challenge in the market place should now be quite clear.

The Salesman as Producer

One aspect which has been touched on could perhaps be amplified if it is desired to explore the selling job further. It has been said that the salesman is employed to get orders, and for many companies he

Table 5.1

Buyclass	*Customer's needs*	*Supplier's Aims*	*Salesman's Success Factors*
Straight Rebuy	Assurance that quality, delivery and price will remain competitive. A channel for complaints or special requests.	*"In" Supplier* To keep customer's loyalty. To increase value of orders.	Regular contact. Good personal relations. Efficient handling of queries and complaints.
		"Out" Supplier To change buying procedure to modified rebuy OR To change customer's working arrangements to create "new buy" situation.	Strong approach. Good product presentation. Ability to create confidence. Knowledge of customer's business.
Modified Rebuy	Information on new product. Proof of its superiority. Assurance that service, delivery, etc., will not suffer by a change of product or supplier.	*"In" Supplier* To increase value of orders. To make modified rebuy a straight rebuy in future.	Applicational knowledge. Regular contact. Good personal relations.
		"Out" supplier To maintain novelty and avoid reversion to old buying practices. To establish status as a regular supplier.	Belief in superiority of product. Knowledge of competition. Detailed attention to customer's needs. Ability to create confidence.
New Buy	A great deal of information on the product and its application. Advice in adapting existing techniques/practices to new product/method. Assurance that selected product is superior to alternatives available. Assurance of after-sales service.	To convince customer of need – or confirm that need is recognized. To eliminate alternative methods of doing the job. To demonstrate that the product will fulfil the customer's requirement. To demonstrate that the product has cost/benefit advantages over competitive offerings. To create confidence in future service.	Detailed knowledge of customer's business. Knowledge of alternative methods/processes. Detailed knowledge of the product. Skill in presentation/demonstration. Knowledge of competition. Knowledge of financial implications of purchase. Ability to create confidence.

is the chief source of business. On his efforts depend the continued well-being of his company and the jobs of other employees. His activities are therefore a matter of keen interest to his employers, and he is measured by the results he achieves. The yardsticks used may often have to be fairly crude — previous turnover from his territory, targets set by management, or the results obtained by other salesmen — but regular measurement is part of a salesman's life. Now there are many occupations you may choose where measurement is applied spasmodically if at all, and where you may hope to "get by" so long as you commit no gross or obvious misdemeanour. For a salesman his figures, weekly, monthly and annually are a matter of record. For many there is a great incentive in having personal achievement identified in this way. But if you are not prepared to be measured, once you have been fully trained and equipped for the job, you should not contemplate selling as a career, or even as a stage in career.

The Salesman's Day

Let us look at a day in the life of a salesman whose work contains a mixture of the aspects we have so far discussed. Our salesman, John Morton, is of course fictitious, although his aims, emotions and experiences are not. John has worked for a company marketing office machinery for a couple of years. After preliminary training at the firm's headquarters and a few weeks "on the road" accompanying more experienced men, he was given a territory of his own in the East Midlands, covering the Leicester and Loughborough area. He is part of a team of five salesmen who report to an Area Sales Manager based on Nottingham. Since being assigned to a territory he has been paid a commission on orders taken in addition to his basic salary. He runs a company car which he can use for private motoring at weekends and during his holidays.

A Demonstration

On a Monday morning John experiences the same feelings that beset the rest of us and getting to work is no easier for him, especially when it involves calling on strangers who may have no wish to hear what he has to say. For this reason John likes to fix his key appointments as early in the morning as possible, to get off to a good start. Today he is due in Loughborough at 9.30 a.m., and this gives him time to telephone his branch office to check whether there are any messages or letters waiting for him. If anything urgent requires his attention he can adjust his plan for the day accordingly or telephone his customers and arrange further appointments. As it is, there is nothing that cannot wait, although he is very pleased to hear that confirmation has now been received of an order he took verbally the previous week.

The 9.30 appointment is to demonstrate his machine to a prospective customer. The night before, John made sure the machine was working properly and stowed it carefully in his car. He has learned by experience that nothing can safely be left to chance. At the customer's office he has to set the machine up, check that it is ready for operation and make sure, as far as he can, that all the people who could influence the buying decision are present for the demonstration. It may be worth noting in passing that John never uses the word "demonstration" when speaking to his customers. He is simply bringing a machine along to show them how it works and how it will do the job they require of it. That is after all what they are buying, not flashy showmanship on his part. All the same, he has practised every action needed to show how easy the machine is to operate and he works to a sequence which presents his product to its best advantage. There is nothing parrot-fashion about his presentation. He changes the sequence whenever he feels it appropriate and looks for any opportunity to relate the features and benefits of his product to his customer's office methods.

In this case John finds he has problems. The demonstration has gone quite smoothly but he finds one departmental manager, who was not present at previous discussions, very hard to convince. John has therefore to resell the value of a change in method as well as to prove that the machine will do all that he has claimed for it. This takes time and stimulates a general argument among departmental heads which results in a decision to postpone final approval until the next board meeting. Then the issue will not be the purchase of a single machine for the Loughborough office, but a change to automation throughout the company, which would require four machines at least.

John is naturally pleased at the prospect of a larger sale, but he had hoped to secure a firm order and is worried by the delay. He knows that even a few weeks' delay can change a customer's circumstances and put what was previously a priority out of mind altogether. There is also a danger that competitors will appear on the scene and benefit from the creative selling he has done. So even while he is packing his machine and preparing to leave, his mind is turning to ways and means of maintaining interest in his proposition. He notes the date of the board meeting and considers how he might refresh the memories of those who will attend. Some additional information or literature presented just beforehand might help. Anyhow, he makes out a full report before making his next call, just to be sure that he forgets nothing of importance.

"Cold Calling"

There are several firms nearby with whom the company is doing no business and John now calls on three of these in an attempt to make contact with the decision-maker and to assess the chances of a sale. For many salesmen "cold calling" of this type is an essential part of their work. This is very much the case in John's business, where potential users are distributed over the whole of industry. The initial approach might be by letter or telephone, but a personal call, in the course of a day's travelling, has the advantage of providing information about the company visited as well as offering the chance of face-to-face contact with a prospective buyer.

On his first call John is unable to see anyone in authority or to find out anything about the present method of operation. He resolves to try a telephone approach next time. The second call is more promising and he secures a firm appointment with the company secretary for his next visit to Loughborough in a week's time. The third is a disappointment. He discovers that a competitor's machine has been purchased and, what is worse, within the last six months. "If we had known you sold this type of equipment we would have been glad to look at your machine." John is not at all happy to be beaten to the punch, so it is in a somewhat chastened mood that he goes to meet his area sales manager for lunch.

The Lunch Problem

Lunch is a problem for salesmen. Of course there are times when it is necessary to entertain important customers but in the type of selling John does, these occasions are rare. Generally, John is looking for somewhere for lunch which is inexpensive and, preferably, non-alcoholic. Not that he does not enjoy a drink, but he feels that his afternoon calls go better if he leaves drinking until the evening; also he is driving. By now he has found a number of suitable places to eat, but the time to eat remains problematical. Most of his potential customers take an hour off for lunch, but which hour? Some may be out from 12 noon to 1 p.m. and others from 1 p.m. to 2 p.m. John cannot afford to sterilize two hours of his working day because of this. The remedy lies partly in knowing his customer's habits, partly in fixing appointments to minimize the time lost.

A Customer's Complaint

Today John and his Sales Manager, Bob White, have an appointment at 2 p.m. sharp with a particularly awkward customer who has not been satisfied with the service he has received. Three months ago John took an order from him in the face of strong competition. He knew at the time that standard delivery was eight weeks, so he promised ten weeks, to allow for any minor problems that might arise. Unfortunately there have since then been production difficulties, due to the failure of a supplier to deliver a vital component. The factory has so far been unable to quote a new date and the customer is threatening to cancel his order and to place all future business elsewhere.

John and Bob discuss the problem over lunch. They could do one of two things: they might offer the B model which lacks some of the features of the machine originally sold, but is available from stock, or they could attempt to persuade the customer that waiting will be worth while. Bob feels that the B model is not right for this application and he knows that his company is taking emergency action to get production moving again. Eventually they decide that they will resell the benefits of their product and persuade the customer to wait a little longer, if they can.

At first this does not appear an easy objective. The customer lets them know in no uncertain fashion exactly what he thinks of broken promises. John is ready to reply but takes his cue from Bob, who simply sits and listens with great attention to everything the customer has to say. He then apologizes for the delay and explains why he thinks the particular machine ordered is ideal for the customer's application. He asks if there is anything he can do to help, by, for example, enlisting the aid of another user in the Loughborough area who may have vacant time on his machine. It emerges that the most urgent job will not be ready to run for another eight weeks. Bob promises to do all he can to obtain a machine by then and to find other ways of helping if by any chance he fails.

Back in the car Bob and John discuss the interview and the lessons to be learned from it. This is a routine they have after every call they make together, and in this case it gives Bob a chance to point out that a salesman who thought his job was talking rather than listening, or who imagined that his work was finished when the order was taken, might have been shown the door. As it is they have every chance of keeping the business and making an enthusiastic and loyal customer out of what had been a justifiably angry man. They both know that ultimately they rely on the factory to solve the production problem, and that there is a limit to anything they can do if deliveries cannot be improved. Bob says he has informed Head Office of the amount of business at stake and that there is every chance they will be out of trouble in a month.

The communication link between buyer and seller at times like this depends very much on the personal relationships each salesman can develop with his own customers, and on the information he can pass back to the company to enable it to fix priorities. John and Bob accept their responsibilities in maintaining this link, although it is not for either of them the most glamorous part of the selling job.

Afternoon Calls

Bob has no intention of ending the day on a low note, and there are several calls still to be made. An hour or so of "cold calling" yields one good prospect worth a second visit. Finally late in the afternoon they visit an existing customer to see that he remains satisfied — and can be quoted as such — and also to see what the chances are of further business. John has heard some talk of expansion and it does seem that more machines could be required within the next six months. Bob has always advised John to make calls of this type later in the day, when hard selling to first-time "prospects" could be more difficult. The atmosphere is relaxed and informal, but the chance of extra business is explored thoroughly.

Summing-Up the Day's Activity

Before they part company the two men review the day's activity. For some time Bob has been concerned that sales in the Loughborough area are few and far between, although John's overall results are good and he is now the second-best producer in the team. It seems to both of them that if things are to improve Loughborough has to be covered more systematically. They agree that the potential for more business exists and that more calls should be made. This, however, is easier said than done. It calls for self-discipline and journey planning if more time is to be spent talking to customers and less flitting by car between Loughborough and Leicester, where business is booming. Bob can offer some help from the sales office in handling Leicester queries so that John can mount his own concentrated campaign, and arranges for them to spend a full day together next week to build up a healthy prospect list.

Of course there is no such thing as an average day, and as has been said there are many kinds of selling job, but the day we have sketched might at least feel familiar to those who have sold to end users in the modified rebuy or new buy situations. What cannot be shown in a bare account of events is the excitement of achieving an order against competition, or the pleasure of seeing your own figures move to the top of the list, or the professional interest of discussing and improving selling or demonstration techniques with your colleagues, or the deep satisfaction that comes from knowing that your customers are convinced they have received value for money. The commission is useful too! But against this the salesman is often working alone and is exposed to disappointment and to complaints as well as to success and the commendation of satisfied customers. He is very much in the position of running his own business on the territory assigned to him, with all the ups and downs that entails. Meeting people and handling their queries and objections is tiring, whatever the results of the encounters may be. At the end of the day the salesman knows he has done a day's work.

We shall shortly discuss the qualities needed to succeed in this kind of work — and to enjoy it. In the meantime it may be wise to explain to anyone who thinks he would feel somewhat naked in John's situation, something of the resources that a salesman working for a reputable company has at his disposal.

Sales Aids — the Salesman's Arms and Armour

In order to be able to fulfil the role outlined in Table 5.1, a salesman requires training. He is not simply given a territory and sent out to do battle. He is provided with information about his product and its uses, about competition and about the methods others have found effective in selling the product. This gives him the confidence to approach customers, knowing that he can offer some at least of the information they require. With success and experience he builds upon this knowledge to become expert in his own field. Naturally it takes time, because he has to see the product used in a variety of ways and to meet a wide range of customers' problems and queries before he knows most of the answers. But solid product knowledge is the prime sales aid.

Allied to this there is the product itself. No one should sell something in which he does not believe. If the product looks good or works well it helps to sell itself. The salesman who can demonstrate its capabilities has the finest imaginable sales aid at his fingertips.

Nevertheless most companies will back the product with literature, advertising or sales promotion of one form or another. This either helps directly in the selling situation or produces enquiries the salesman can follow up. With the odd enquiry coming in, the day never feels quite so "cold".

Finally there are existing customers, themselves the source of enquiries, and a steady support to the salesman, assuring him by their satisfaction that what he is selling is good, and that he has every right to bring his product to the attention of those who might need it.

So the salesman is very far from naked when he knocks at a new door. He has tested his arms and armour in a number of previous encounters and knows they are the best that he and his company can devise. Given that an application exists, he knows he has a solid chance of success.

Selling as a Career

The Time to Enter

It is not always possible to enter selling direct from school or college. The reason for this is related to our earlier analysis of the sales function. What customers want from a salesman is information, advice or assurance. It is hardly likely that you will be able to provide this without first acquiring some background in commerce, industry, or at least life outside the academic world. What you can do is to choose your earlier jobs with an eye to gathering the experience you will need as a salesman.

The appropriate background varies according to the type of selling you have in mind. Previous work in laboratories or engineering shops may well help those whose job it is to sell to chemists, doctors, scientists or engineers. Experience of agriculture — or the lack of it — will soon show if you attempt to sell to farmers. Our "typical" salesman, John Morton, may have worked in a sales office, thus acquiring a knowledge of office administration, as well as soaking up the atmosphere of a selling environment. Younger people can often benefit from tackling internal selling jobs, or customer service functions, before going out to find customers of their own. Good administration, whether in writing reports, completing orders or handling customers' queries, is important in field selling as well as in the office, and the sooner it is mastered the better. For overseas selling any job which develops your ability to speak other languages will pay dividends later.

Channels of Promotion

Good salesmen are comparatively rare, and are generally well rewarded by commission or bonus. Many therefore prefer to stay as salesmen rather than climb the ladder of management. Anyone looking for career development, however, has a number of options, once he has proved himself in the field.

We have already had a glimpse of an area sales manager at work. To run a small team of salesmen is the first step in field management, but it is not a small or insignificant step. The difference for the successful salesman is not money. In any given month, or year, the area sales manager may not earn as much as his top salesman — this depends on the type of commission scheme in force — although he will usually do better than the average member of his team. The real change is one common to all promotions to management level, and that is acceptance of one's reliance on the efforts of others. This is perhaps even more of a step in selling than elsewhere, because a salesman has so great a degree of freedom in his day-to-day activity. Then suddenly, as a manager, he finds himself dependent on the work of others who are just as individualistic in their jobs as he was in his. He can give advice or instructions but he has no *direct* means of ensuring that his advice is taken. He cannot be with all his men on every call. Sales management therefore demands leadership as much as, and possibly more than, any other management job. The sales manager has to convince his team that his selling ideas and methods — or those they construct between them — are the surest route to success. What is more he has frequently to show that they work in the field, by selling in front of the most critical audience he could have, his own salesmen.

As a sales manager progresses up the ladder, field work has to yield ground to those elements of planning and control which affect the economics of the sales operation. The national sales manager is concerned with the overall size of his sales force, where salesmen should best be deployed, what selling methods should be adopted, what incentives should be given, and what results can be expected. At this point selling and marketing planning tend to merge, and, according to circumstances, a variety of further promotions are possible — sales director, marketing director or perhaps chief executive.

For those with an interest in marketing planning or sales promotion an earlier transition might be made from line to functional management. The path to wider responsibilities might then lead through product management, market research, sales training, or perhaps the management of a small, specialized division. In some firms there are opportunities for those who can handle the larger customers as national accounts managers or as managers of departments dealing with specific categories of business such as export or government sales. Indeed, export selling as part of international marketing is becoming increasingly a major function in its own right.

There are therefore many paths a selling career may take and there is no reason why a salesman should not reach the top of his chosen organization. In a world market which grows increasingly competitive it would seem desirable that more top executives should have had sales experience at some time in their careers than is the case at present.

The Qualities Needed for Success

There are as yet no tests that can identify potential sales ability with any degree of certainty. The problem is that there are too many variables in selling to make it possible to match human personality consistently with the requirements of the job. One person may therefore succeed in a given type of selling where another fails, and vice versa. This is another reason why entry into selling can seldom be your first job. It takes time to get to know yourself in the world of business. When you have found your feet it may be easier to recognize the selling role you will find most congenial and in which you are most likely to succeed.

Nevertheless the work that has been put into devising tests and studying the personality profiles of successful salesmen has not been entirely in vain and some generalizations can be made.

For example the salesman must obviously be able to identify with the problems and attitudes of his prospective customers. A genuine interest in people and a certain amount of empathy is required. Nevertheless by itself this would not generate business. However much customers liked a salesman, they would not be persuaded to buy without some firmness on his part. People sometimes need a push before coming to a buying decision, and the salesman often has to give this, if only by opening his mouth and asking for the order. So the will to win must be present and an attitude which does not easily take "no" for an answer. When this is not balanced by empathy, selling can become over-aggressive, but without a great deal of determination no salesman will succeed in the modified rebuy or new buy situation, however pleasant a personality he may have.

Given these basic qualities, it must next be recognized that customers do not want just empathy, nor do they always appreciate having their minds made up for them. What they want is information. They want to deal with someone who knows what he is talking about and can advise them how they can benefit by using his product. This implies a detailed product and applicational knowledge in addition to the right personal characteristics.

Knowledge of this kind, in sufficient depth to be effective, requires a good deal of work. Everything relevant to the product and its market has to be learned and it cannot always be learned behind a desk. What customers value, and how they use a given product is discovered by meeting them, listening to what they have to say and studying how they run their businesses. Some patience and determination is needed as well as a genuine interest in your chosen field of operation. Which all adds up to hard work, but not uninteresting work. The successful salesman just cannot be bored in his job.

The capacity to work is required not only to master all facets of the product and its applications but also to make the right number of calls. However clever a salesman may be he has to expose himself and his product to the risk of success, and this means calls and yet more calls. All other things being equal, a hard-working, knowledgable salesman will produce business where his more brilliant and less organized colleague fails, simply by placing himself in front of prospective customers more often.

To do this requires self-discipline and resilience to accept the setbacks and rebuffs which are inevitable with so high a degree of exposure to a sceptical market. Does this mean that the hard-working salesman who maintains a good calling rate is thick-skinned? To believe that is to accept one of the common anti-selling myths we identified at the beginning of this chapter. The best salesmen are able to accept failure when it comes their way as a statistical fact, just as a first-class sportsman knows he cannot win all the time. This is maturity, not insensitivity. But it must be admitted that a well-developed sense of humour helps on occasion.

If and when you feel you have these qualities, an attempt to master the skills of selling should prove beneficial, whether you stay in the selling field or subsequently move on to other jobs in business. So much these days has to be achieved through persuasion. In management we are always having to convince others that what we propose is right for the situation in which we find ourselves. A professional, salesmanlike approach will generally prove more effective than arguments or bullying. It will also create a better working atmosphere where continuing business relationships are involved. For this reason it is probably true to say that those of us who have been salesmen never stop selling.

6. Advertising

David Wheeler

Suppose you have something to sell – you want to find as many buyers as you can. You might put a card in a newsagent's window or you could tell your friends about it. But a far more effective way might be to insert a small advertisement in your local paper which will be seen by thousands of people instead of a score or two.

The same thing applies in the business world. Many firms have found that advertising usually offers an effective and economical way of selling their goods whether to High Street shoppers or to buyers of industrial machinery.

In 1985 approximately £4,441 million was spent on all forms of advertising. About forty per cent went on consumer advertising – the commercials on TV and radio, press and magazine advertisements, posters – the rest on advertisements for industrial equipment and for banks and insurance companies, and small three-or-four-line "classified" advertisements.

Although this seems a vast sum it is less than two per cent of total consumer expenditure. And it should be remembered that manufacturers are not the only people who spend money on consumer advertising.

Thus advertising is all part of the marketing and selling process – whether for a product or service or for getting across an idea to change attitudes. Advertising is a hard commercial business, offering a challenging and rewarding career to young people who have a strong business sense or outstanding creative talents. But it has little to offer people who, even if they are artistically inclined, do not want to become involved with the commercial world.

If you are thinking of a career at the core of business; if you enjoy working with quick imaginative people; if you are resilient and have the ability to solve problems under pressure; if you believe that selling things is just as important as making them; then you are right to consider a job in advertising. Within advertising there are innumerable different careers open to you: you might want to join, for example, the advertisement department of a newspaper or television company; you may prefer to start on the client side with a big advertiser; or you may set your sights on an advertising agency.

Before going on to the various parts of the advertising industry I should first explain what advertising is and how it works.

What is Advertising?

The primary purpose of advertising is to sell goods and services at a profit to the company supplying them. Advertisements offer a wide range of suggestions or pieces of information to people so that they can make up their minds which product to buy or which service to use. They first *inform* the buyer of what is available and the price and secondly they usually include a persuasive selling message.

"Persuasion" in advertising can be in two forms – a "hard sell", especially appropriate for those products where consumer benefits can be readily demonstrated, or "soft-sell" where the emphasis is on atmosphere and association, but which nevertheless stresses product advantages. It's no use if the reader or viewer just remembers galloping horses on a seashore and forgets the brand name!

Advertising is used to keep established brands fresh in the minds of customers. Once advertising stops, demand for the product begins to fall away. It is also used for launching new products and for informing customers of improvements to existing lines.

Clearly then, advertising is an essential part of marketing, helping to stimulate demand (thereby increasing production) and providing jobs through increased sales.

Advertising in the Marketing Context

The advertiser's message is established in the consumer's mind because it is memorable and frequently exposed. That is the basic underlying principle of advertising. Marketing identifies the sections of the population which are the potential customers for the advertised brand – what we call the target group. In the case of a detergent, for instance or it could mean virtually all housewives in the country; if it were a motor-car then the advertisement would often be aimed principally at men; if it were a mobile crane, then it would only be of interest to the construction industry; and if it were a light aircraft then it would only appeal to a tiny minority.

Great care, therefore, has to be taken to ensure that the advertising is directed at the right target group and the advertiser uses the advertising agency to define, through its marketing expertise, precisely the right audience and the most appropriate, cost-effective medium, be it a national newspaper, a regional TV station or a professional journal circulating to engineers, for instance.

Expenditure on advertising must make a positive contribution to the advertiser's profits and, as it is part of its total expenditure, a company must earn a return on its advertising investment. Therefore the size of the budget has to be carefully related to the market potential and the particular marketing goals.

How that money is spent depends on a number of factors: the media to be used, the creative requirements, the number of times the advertisement is to appear and so on. It is the advertising agency's job to decide the marketing strategy in consultation with the advertiser and then to devise a campaign to meet the marketing objectives within the limits of the budget.

Advertising is an integral part of the total marketing effort. Its effectiveness will depend not only on the persuasiveness of the selling message and the accuracy of pin-pointing the target groups but on product and market research, production, sales and distribution, and financial control.

What are things which advertising *cannot* do? It cannot sell a product that doesn't offer value or which doesn't live up to the claims made for it. The consumer will never buy a useless or over-priced product twice!

On its own, advertising cannot make instant sales; it takes time to build brand loyalty – and advertising usually has to be continuous to work properly; it is a long-term investment. And advertising cannot sell products which are not available in shops where they are normally expected to be found.

Structure of the Business

Advertisers, agencies and newspapers, magazines, television and radio companies, poster contractors and supply houses all have their own trade organizations representing their interests which are joined together under the umbrella of the Advertising Association, the representative organization putting forward the "public face" of advertising.

Advertisers belong to the Incorporated Society of British Advertisers (ISBA) which currently has over 2,000 member companies. The Institute of Practitioners in Advertising (the IPA), representing the advertising agencies, has a corporate membership of about 250 agencies, as well as some 1,600 qualified individual members employed in those agencies. These IPA agencies account for eighty per cent of the advertising placed on behalf of advertisers.

The Newspaper Publishers Association represents the interests of national newspapers and the Newspaper Society covers the regional press. Television contractors belong to the Independent Television Companies Association and commercial radio stations to the Association of Independent Radio Contractors. Posters, cinema and direct mail have their own trade associations.

All advertisers and agencies have to adhere to the strict provisions of the British Code of Advertising Practice. This is administered by the Advertising Standards Authority which investigates complaints from the public about any press, poster or cinema advertisements which infringe the Code. ASA also enforces the British Code of Sales Promotion Practice. Television and radio commercials are governed by the statutory Code operated by the Independent Broadcasting Authority. All commercials have to be carefully vetted before they can be transmitted.

There are hundreds of different jobs one could choose in advertising. We shall discuss here the three main sides of advertising – the advertisers, agencies and media – how they work and the kind of jobs that you might expect to do.

Advertisers

Most big companies – particularly those making fast-moving

consumer goods – have an advertising or publicity department which works in close liaison with the firm's appointed advertising agency (or agencies). The advertising department, which is usually linked with part of the marketing department, varies in size according to the scale of the company's output and the services it offers. It might have a total staff of 100 or more if it employs artists, copywriters and photographers, or more usually it would be a small unit of six or seven concerned with budgeting control and media planning. The responsibilities of the department will probably include such things as agreement with management on advertising strategies and objectives; the preparation of advertising plans; selection of advertising agencies, art and photographic studios, printers and designers; and the briefing and supervision of both internal and external services needed for the execution of advertising plans.

Whether the company is big or small, the number of executive posts open to graduate trainees rarely exceeds three or four. Ultimately the trainee will aspire to the position of Brand Manager who prepares the annual marketing plan and is responsible for all aspects of advertising and promotion for a particular product or group of products. Either as an advertising executive or as Brand Manager or even Marketing Director, you are in an excellent position to move over to a job in an advertising agency on the account service side.

A job in the marketing department of a large manufacturing company provides many opportunities for rapid career advancement. Hear how Frank Vymetal, a marketing manager with Beecham Proprietaries, started in advertising.

"To have taken degrees in operational research and then finished up in marketing must be a strange career path, but it was only when doing a further degree in operational research that I realized my interests would be best served by operating in a line management role, rather than progressing with a career in a pure service function.

"So why marketing? Like many others, I would suspect, my interest stemmed from an engaging course at university which showed me that marketing was more than just producing a television commercial, or selling a product to the trade. Marketing seemed to offer the opportunity of liaising with a number of departments within an organization and also reporting directly to management, thereby providing a direct contribution to a part of the business.

"I joined Beecham directly from university and was then attached to the marketing department as a trainee, working in the haircare group. Although there was no formal training programme (Beecham believed in training through involvement at that time), I found that through immediate involvement I was learning fast about the world of commercial marketing. After a year I was moved to the dentifrice group, to give me greater responsibility and to broaden my experience. I was involved in the re-launch of Aquafresh toothpaste and was then given responsibility for Vosene shampoo, the hair colourant brands and later the Airwick range of products. I am now in the medicine division.

"I have had a high level of job rotation when compared to other fields, but not uncommon amongst marketing people. The rotation, I believe, is beneficial because it gives the chance to gain experience within a number of product fields and to encounter the problems related to those fields/brands.

"My first few years of marketing convinced me that I was right to change my 'career plan' and that marketing was not a 9–5 desk-bound job, but more importantly it enabled me to come into contact with levels of management and to witness tangible evidence of my contribution to the company."

Another equally important aspect of the company's marketing operation is the research department, embracing product and consumer research which provides the Brand Manager with the necessary information to determine marketing strategy. This might include an analysis of such factors as the present product range, market trends, consumer attitudes, prices and competitors.

In these instances, it is the job of the Brand Manager or Advertising Manager to interpret the research information for the formulation of the advertising plan. It is at this point that the advertising agency takes over.

The Advertising Agency

The purpose of the advertising agency is to provide additional and special skills. Some agencies may have as many as 60 or more separate client companies between them selling anything up to 150 different products, so working in an agency is a first-class way to gain broad knowledge of the business world. If you join an agency on the account service side, you will have to get to know as much as possible about your client's business. You will have to evaluate actual and potential markets, work out strategies and budgets and be responsible for all stages of the advertising campaign right from creative concept through to production of the finished press advertisement or TV or radio commercial.

At the centre of operations of most agencies is the Account Director who, with overall responsibility for a number of accounts, is in continuous discussion with his clients about the broad objectives and progress of advertising campaigns. Then there is the account executive who is concerned with the day-to-day running of the account. This involves the preparation of a detailed specification of a client's needs, their interpretation in terms of advertising action and the briefing of the various departments within the agency, such as the creative team and media planners and the harnessing and encouragement of those resources in pursuit of the advertising objective. The account executive must also study the progress of competitors' campaigns and be ready to advise his client on new product development, when a new product should be launched and how it should be presented.

The Media Department

This has two broad functions – planning the media schedule (how many press or television advertisements, in which medium and how often) and buying space or time at the most economical rates. Having received a brief from the account executive, who gives information on target audiences and the budget limitations, the planners and buyers use research data on press readership and television viewing patterns to determine which newspaper or magazine to use, or which television or radio station and at what frequency and time.

Prices vary considerably: for instance, in 1987 the cost of a full-page advertisement in the *Daily Express* was about £25,000 compared with £4,280 in the *Birmingham Mail*, and yet because of their different readerships the cost of reaching *Birmingham Mail* readers is more than doubled. In television, a 30-second commercial on the week-day London station Thames TV screened during the peak viewing time between 6.30pm and 7.30pm would cost £35,000, whereas a similar spot on Anglia would cost under £8,000. But again as there are far more viewers in London than in Anglia region, the relative cost of reaching the Thames audience is correspondingly lower.

As examples show, media planning and research is largely statistical, and media executives must be numerate, skilled in analytical techniques and have a sound commercial sense with the ability to relate marketing plans and creative requirements to available media.

Media buying is primarily a commercial function, usually involving hard bargaining with the advertisement departments of newspapers and television companies to secure the best deal for the advertiser. Besides requiring an intimate knowledge of the media available, media buyers work under extreme pressure and therefore need stamina coupled with a sound business sense.

Their job is an extremely important one and it is quite common for media buyers still in their twenties to be responsible for budgets running into several millions of pounds.

The Creative Department

Let us look now at the other major side of the agency, the creative department, on which the success of the campaign – and very often the agency itself – largely depends.

A job in this department demands an ability to think creatively, and to express this creativity in getting across the advertiser's message succinctly, clearly and with a degree of persuasion that will encourage the reader or viewer to buy the advertised product.

The creative department, which is run by a creative director and group heads, employs copywriters, who write the advertisements, and artists and typographers who are responsible for the look of the advertisement and produce the finished work for reproduction in the newspaper or magazine.

There are also scriptwriters and producers who work on television and radio commercials. (The actual production is usually carried out by a specialist company).

Besides being imaginative and able to write well and convincingly, copywriters must be interested in products and people. The best ideas seldom come from flashes of inspiration (although many a copywriter has claimed that he thinks up his best ideas in the bath!). They are normally the result of painstaking thought and discussion with the client and other people in the agency. Only the very talented will succeed, and remember that there are a very few of them – under five per cent of the total employed.

IPA Agencies

An advertising agency earns its income from planning, creating, producing and placing advertisements. It normally receives a commission of fifteen per cent from the media owners, or it may work on a fee basis.

The 250 agencies who are members of the Institute of Practitioners in Advertising were responsible in 1986 for a total advertising investment of more than £3,000 million representing eight-five to ninety per cent of all UK advertising placed by UK advertising agencies. They employ some 13,500 people, from managing director to liftman. It is thus a small business in terms of numbers employed and competition for jobs is stiff; only the very talented or those with previous experience on the client side will have much chance of getting in.

Many Different Jobs

However, having sounded that warning note, there are many different jobs you can do in an agency (if you develop the right qualifications and experience) ranging from copywriting and media planning to production and research. Some young people start off in "traffic" (the progress department) and can go on to join the client service side in a junior capacity. Once that hurdle is crossed, you are well on the road to becoming an account executive. Success as an account person can often lead on to a management position with special responsibilities for servicing major accounts.

The advertising agency is a high-speed business, demanding great attention to detail. Agencies are generally less formal than other firms, but they require above average stability of character, level of intelligence, thoroughness and the ability to withstand pressure. People in agencies work long hours – often weekends – but the rewards, both financial and in job satisfaction, are high, especially in the senior positions which are often reached at a surprisingly young age.

When a company appoints an agency, it is in some ways rather like going to a solicitor for legal advice. The advertiser looks to his agency for a professional service – in the sense that it is something that he cannot do for himself – which calls for special skills and a wide range of experience.

Some Personal Views

Let's hear what it is like working in an agency from four people who started at the bottom a short while ago and are now well on the way towards senior positions.

First, Michael Llewellyn-Williams, who, at 27, was an account manager with advertising agency Boase Massimi Pollitt Univas Partnership:

"Advertising was just one of three careers I was offered during the final stages of a 'brilliant' (not my word!) PhD thesis on vapour transport in polymeric membranes at Imperial College, London. The also-rans were stockbroking (good prospects, but too dry) and marketing in industry (tempting salary, but too stratified and too much bureaucracy).

"The common factor which had led me to consider each of the three in the first instance was pressure – the kind that's caused by having bags of work to be done and deadlines to be achieved in a very short time. I had discovered, three years previously, that I thrived on pressure by running a college newspaper full-time for twelve months – often working 60–70 hours per week to produce *Felix* every Friday. Moving from polymer science into advertising, then, was not so much switching *out* of my field as switching *back* to the world of media.

"In my future career as an account man, I expect advertising to push me to my limit; that's something I wish to discover. Financial reward comes a fair but definite second to the prime target of the personal satisfaction to be gained from surviving the sheer volatility and the ubiquitous tightrope exercises the industry seems to be full of!

"Perhaps most important of all, advertising will give me the opportunity to work with all sorts of products and businesses; and by becoming fully involved with companies' marketing strategies and developments I hope to be able to contribute positively to their overall profitability and success."

Stephen Fox, who, at 28, was an Associate Director at Geers

Gross Advertising, started in the legal profession, but preferred the excitements of advertising. Here is his story.

"It is probably a unique feature of the advertising agency business that no-one really sets out to become an 'Advertising Person' – in fact, they are more likely to find themselves in it by chance or luck.

"All right, I admit that there are those who, on leaving school or university, decide to become an account man, but the number of people who originally set out on careers that could not be further from advertising is quite extraordinary.

"I know of ex-teachers, lawyers, researchers, chemists and even an archaeologist who at some time found that this strange and often bizarre business offered more stimulation, excitement and personal job satisfaction (as well as being well-paid) than the careers they had planned or worse, someone else had planned for them.

"As for myself, I was to be the most successful criminal lawyer of the 80s – the Lord Denning of the working classes – the classic boy made good – and my parents and school were expecting the same. Yet after two years in law, nine months as an Articled Clerk and the rest at law school, I realized that there really had to be more to life than Land Acts relating to Mediaeval Custom and a snail in a lemonade bottle as a precedent for court action.

"That may sould glib but it *was* a difficult decision, not just because of the implications of breaking Articles, but also because of the disappointment my family would experience.

"I discovered advertising because the Youth Employment Office couldn't discover any suitable job for me. I remember a friend suggesting that somebody must make these 30-second horror films that sell green soap (or was it peas?) and that it might just be a career that could satisfy an ex-lawyer who had asked the employment office for the sort of job they did not believe existed in the world, let alone in Lewisham.

"Thirty individually typed letters later, 14 interviews, three offers of a job and having developed an interview technique that was second to none – I was in.

"But I didn't know what I was in for. Six months production, six months media and then I was called a junior account executive which sounded quite impressive until I realized that the word 'junior' was the most important of the three.

"Still, I have moved on, and fortunately up, and 'junior' has disappeared to be replaced by 'senior' – though I still have a few years to retirement, unless, of course, the Managing Director thinks differently.

"The business is frustrating, unglamorous and gives you headaches. It upsets the wife and kids, and sometimes your stomach (not necessarily in that order). Yet the people (and I include the client) are unique; they stimulate you, they force you to think for yourself, they rely on you and you on them. It can be overwhelmingly exciting when new business is won or a campaign is accepted, and soul-destroying when it is lost.

"The work changes every day, sometimes (though fortunately not often) so do the people, but nobody *works* for advertising – you have to live it.

"You cannot explain to outsiders why you get a thrill from a successful launch of frozen chickens, but you do and I'm convinced that there is no other industry that has more dedicated, forceful, caring individuals than advertising, unless of course you've heard a rumour that the legal profession is entering the twentieth-century."

And now hear how Clive Warries, who, at 24, was a media planner at Everetts started:

"I entered this business four years ago having been accepted for a position in the media department of a London advertising agency advertised in an evening newspaper. It was one of the first salaried jobs I'd applied for having been out of school for two months and failing to make a fortune selling encyclopaedias. Knowing how difficult it is to get into this business nowadays I guess I was lucky to do so easily.

"When I started I had little idea what the business was all about but now I can think of few other careers which I could have chosen which would have been so enjoyable.

"It's a very social business and I've met a variety of real characters from many different sides of the business. Getting to know each of them has given me a wide outlook on life and has given me an outgoing personality.

"Advertising has enabled me to develop many of my talents, some of which I didn't know I had. I'm acquiring a good knowledge of commerce and business procedure; I've learnt to watch closely what's going on in the outside world, especially if it affects the economy as this can affect the fortunes of the agency and maybe my job. If I ever wanted to start my own business I've got the background for a good start.

"The aspect I find particularly attractive about this career is that there is no set progression up the job promotion ladder. It's up to the individual to advance himself and it is quite possible if one has the right abilities and has made the right moves at the right time to reach a very lucrative and prominent position by your early thirties.

"This I find a big incentive to work hard and it is reassuring to know that if I do as well as I think I can then in a couple of years I could be living very comfortably and considering buying my first property, which is a great hurdle in anyone's life."

What does an agency look for in a candidate seeking a job in an agency?

Let's hear from a personnel manager from one of London's leading agencies:

"Last year between December and March we received applications from over 800 university graduates seeking a career in advertising. We were looking for four Account Service trainees and so we were faced with a huge task of selecting those best few candidates.

"We responded by asking people to write to us answering a set of questions that we would normally cover during an initial interview. The obvious question was 'Why do you want a career in advertising?' followed of course, by 'Why do you want to join our agency?'.

"We sorted through response after response and found that people had very set ideas about what advertising will offer them.

"Of course, it is difficult to generalize, but what we saw were many applicants who believed that advertising will give them the freedom they can't find in a large bureaucratic organization. They believe that in a good advertising agency they can make good money, advance rapidly if they do a good job, meet lots of creative, influential and interesting people, and best of all, enjoy the excitement that comes from creating TV and cinema commercials.

"For those people who choose an advertising rather than a marketing career, their decision is based on a desire to have lots of variety in their future career. They want to have contact with many different clients. They want to be involved with different product lines. They want a chance to express themselves in a wide variety of ways which they don't believe is possible in a purely marketing function.

"From the other side, most applicants feel that they bring to the business a talent for expressing themselves; they feel they are good organizers, can get along well with all kinds of people, have keen imaginations and can come up with creative ideas that will sell.

"At the end of the day, it is this last point which is critical for us; we hire people who we believe can come up with a distinctive creative solution to the client's problem; a solution that the client will buy; and, of course, a solution that will sell more of the product to the consumer.

"What we look for when we hire someone is that something extra in intelligence, in personality, in common sense, in advertising insight. Probably the most important attribute we seek is a real keenness to make a career in advertising, because we believe that aside from having talent, you must be willing to work very hard to succeed in our business."

Special Functions by Agencies

Some agencies concentrate on industrial advertising, others on recruitment and financial advertising. But they all operate in much the same way: the only real difference is that the people they employ – especially on the creative and media side – have specialist knowledge of the particular fields in which they are working. For instance, a copywriter working on an industrial account has to have some technical or mechanical knowledge; media planners and buyers need to be well acquainted with the trade and professional press. Special skills, too, are needed by copywriters working in recruitment advertising and, of course, a person working on a financial account should ideally have a working knowledge of the City.

It should be emphasized that not all people entering agencies are graduates: the majority are not. Many of the most senior people in the business today reached their positions by sheer hard work, starting off as a messenger or office boy.

Working in Press and Television

Newspapers and Magazines

Essentially, there are two main types of jobs on the advertising side of the print media; space selling (either display or classified) and marketing (promotion and circulation). Mostly, these departments are separate units but sometimes, especially in regional newspapers, they are under one head. Some of the bigger publishing groups – the Thomson Organization for example – operate trainee schemes, but these are mainly for graduates. After a period in the display, classified and sales departments a trainee could expect to move on quite quickly to a general management position. Much the same applies in magazine publishing where the biggest organization is the International Publishing Corporation. IPC also operate a training scheme; some people are trained as advertisement executives for a single magazine within the organization while others are trained to deal with specific product groups.

The number of openings for programmed training in any one year is limited, and is unlikely to exceed ten at the most. Whether a graduate or not, publishing is hard to get into and only the really persistent will succeed! Nevertheless, there are more openings in publishing than in the agency business, so you might find a newspaper or magazine a good place to start, so long as you are prepared to begin at the bottom.

Someone who did just that is Andrew Pike, who gained his early experience first at *The Sunday Telegraph* and then as an advertising sales executive with Mirror Group Newspapers. He says that for an undergraduate the selection of a career is probably the single most important decision of his college life. Theoretically the options are endless, but when examined they can appear dramatically finite. For him advertising emerged as the natural choice.

He writes: "As an undergraduate studying for a BA Hons degree in English/History but not wanting a teaching post or an academic career, I thought that there was no choice but to go into business. But lack of knowledge about the commercial world can make it a terrifying prospect. Business is blurred in the mind of the arts student who has been sheltered from the real world by our educational system; blurred and inextricably bound up with industry. Industry which is boring, industry which is about nuts and bolts, facts and figures, and regards people as second-rate machines.

"However, after discussions with my careers department and conversations with a former student who had gone into advertising, I did some research which indicated that the advertising industry might be the ideal combination of business and creativity for which I was searching. I had always had an affinity for the media and particularly towards Fleet Street, and thought that advertising was a poor second to journalism. Not so, advertising carried in the national press is equally important as the editorial content of the paper. Advertising is naturally competitive, obviously creative, definitely contemporary and presents the ideal opportunity for involvement with the scientific and artistic sides of industry.

"Having set my sights on getting into advertising either on the agency or media-owner side I soon discovered that the task of getting accepted was as fiercely competitive as the business itself. Job number one: sell yourself to the employer.

"I wrote letters to the top twenty London agencies, to several publications and media houses. I canvassed the recruitment sections of the trade papers like *Campaign* and *UK Press Gazette* and for my efforts received several interviews which produced several polite refusals. Eventually I was accepted by *The Sunday Telegraph* having followed up an advertisement from their situations vacant columns.

"Once in, I really began to learn what competition was all about. And that facts and figures are just as important as people and personality. However, the excitement of being involved in a contemporary business with the directive to liaise between advertising agencies, their clients, and a national newspaper, I found both stimulating and rewarding."

Television

Getting a job in a television company can be even harder! Over the last few years there has been little expansion in the advertising departments of the major TV contractors and on average sales staffs number about fifty.

Says Derek Stephenson, former Sales Controller of Thames Television: "With the introduction of a sales-based computer system, where TV airtime is sold direct from a video display unit, the number of sales staff, including those engaged on research and marketing services, dropped by about twenty per cent. Nowadays sales executives spend much of their time selling by telephone whereas in the old days they were out and about much more.

Representation out in the field is now mainly at more senior levels in the sales structure."

He says that, on the whole, extensive training facilities are rare and usually it is only people who have some previous experience in advertising who have much chance of getting a job straight away at sales executive level. "However, there is room for people without any previous experience, but they have to start right at the bottom of the ladder."

There are sometimes vacancies in commercial radio, but as with television, opportunities are few and there is little chance of getting organized training.

Conclusion

Advertising offers a worthwhile, varied and challenging career. It is difficult to break into if you are inexperienced. But nothing in this world is impossible if you are really determined. Good luck!

7. Market Research

Christopher West

Research is an overworked term in modern business. Before making almost any decisions whether relating to corporate strategy, investment, product development or marketing communications, a manager requires information and to obtain it he has to carry out or commission some form of research exercise. Research can range in scale from a few hurried calculations on the back of an envelope to years of intensive effort involving teams of highly trained technicians. It can cover any aspect of an organization's activities. Marketing research is that branch of the research business which studies customers and is concerned with the improvement of the quality of marketing decisions. Just as marketing in total is concerned with all those activities concerned with the purchase and sale of goods and services in industrial, institutional and consumer markets and between organizational buyers and sellers, marketing research concerns itself with the gathering, recording and analysis of all facts about problems relating to the transfer and sale of goods from producer to consumer.

But it doesn't quite stop there. Over the years the sampling and other data collection techniques that have been developed for the analysis of customers' behaviour have been applied to a wide range of other applications. These include the determination of political opinions and voting intentions (the opinion polls so widely quoted at election times), the generation of social and related statistics (such as demographic data, expenditure intentions). Furthermore, market research executives have been increasingly called upon to provide general and supportive information not derived from studies of customers but nevertheless required for market planning.

This includes general economic data, forecasts of economic

growth, analyses of political conditions, information on technical specifications, legislation affecting markets and trends in international trade. The market researcher thus lives in a very varied world and his activities relate to most aspects of business life. He may appear to operate in an ivory tower on the touchline of companies' principal activities but in fact the data he provides is used at the very centre of decision-making and large sums of money can hinge on the accuracy of his results.

Major Research Types

Most professions tend over time to develop specialist segments and market research is no exception. Just as the medical profession is divided into surgeons, skin specialists, neurologists, renal specialists and a host of others, the general term "market research" conceals a whole host of research types. The following paragraphs describe some of the more important divisions which can affect a career in the market research business.

The first division to understand is that which distinguishes *qualitative* from *quantitative* research. The most commonly seen research data is in the form of numbers; proportions of the population preferring brand X, the percentage of voters who will vote "yes" or "no" or who don't know, the numbers viewing a particular television programme. Research tends to be highly statistical and the casual observer could be forgiven for thinking that it is all quantitative. In fact this is far from the case. Much research is carried out to identify attitudes, preferences, purchasing practices, readership habits and other "soft" information and the answers may be expressed in a series of qualitative statements about market conditions rather than numbers. Some studies combine the quantitative and the qualitative approach so that the report contains both statistics on market size and brand share with an analysis of why customers prefer one brand to another and how they select their suppliers. Among the research agencies you will find quantitative specialists working with large samples of individuals and households, and qualitative specialists working in the more rarefied atmosphere of the group discussion and psychological tests.

A whole host of further specializations have developed out of the various *objectives* for research exercises. In the space available here we can do little more than list the better-known types but it should be evident that each relates to a very specific part of the overall marketing function. Surveys may be aimed at identifying customer behaviour (the type of research popularized in the writings of Vance Packard) and customers' attitudes towards products, services or suppliers. Media research, advertising research and readership research are related in their examination of the methods by which marketing departments do, or could more effectively, communicate with their customers. Opinion polling is aimed specifically at examining political opinions, while image research is concerned with understanding what customers really feel about products and/or their suppliers. Awareness studies measure whether the manufacturers' messages are getting through and distribution studies look at the physical movement of goods from suppliers to customer. Pricing research is concerned not only with the prices being paid for products but also the customer's perception of the price/value relationship and the impact of price changes on volumes purchased. Packaging research studies the effect of packaging on sales and can be used to determine the most suitable and effective type, shape or colour of packaging to be utilized.

As if the above were not sufficient, further areas of specialization arise out of the sectors of activity which are studied. The customer in the shop is far from being the only object of study even though more money is spent on studying her habits and requirements than on anyone else's. Significant sums of money are also spent on researching professional buyers such as farmers, doctors, manufacturing firms, service industries, financial institutions, government departments, commercial establishments, and institutions such as hospitals and prisons. Specialized branches of research are also concerned with the examination of transportation and leisure. The clearest division lies between consumer research, which as its name implies, is concerned with the study of individuals, and industrial research which looks at organizational markets. Superficially the two are very similar since the same broad techniques are used but, in fact, there are major differences in both the types of information sought and the uses to which they are put. Suffice it to say here that the industrial researcher is often less sophisticated in his use of research techniques largely because industrial markets do not easily lend themselves to the refined sampling and analysis methods adopted in more homogenous consumer markets. However, the industrial researcher may be deeply involved in the solution of a specific marketing problem rather than a simple provider of information and his work therefore, tends to contain a higher component of marketing consultancy than is normally found in the consumer research world.

Data collection techniques also clearly differentiate sectors of the market research business. As we will see later all research relies on some form of interrogation of a sample of customers or potential customers, but the ways in which the interrogation techniques are applied determine the type of research operation. The most common research unit works on individual problems on an *ad hoc* basis, commissioning the required numbers of interviews according to the nature of the problem. In the case of qualitative research use may be made of group discussions or hall tests in addition to or instead of individual interviews. But the *ad hoc* survey is not always the most efficient way of collecting data and in response to manufacturers' demands for data which is collected regularly and is comparable over time, a number of continuous surveys have been established. The most important of these are the consumer panels, which week by week, or month by month, report individual household purchases and the regular retail audits of samples of shops. Data collected from shops is clearly different from that collected directly from the customer but each have their uses in marketing. As with *ad hoc* surveys, panel members may be asked to provide their data in a variety of ways. For example, some television audience statistics are collected automatically by a meter fixed to the back of a sample of sets. Other panels report by means of a diary or through an interviewer who calls at regular intervals to collect the information.

The essential difference between the panel research specialists and *ad hoc* research companies is one of scale. Establishing and running a panel of 30,000 housewives, for example, requires an extremely large research operation with a clear division of labour between statisticians, fieldwork, data processing and the sale of results. The staff of such companies normally specialize in one of the major functions and rarely change course. The typical *ad hoc* research company is relatively small and staff tend to be "jacks of all trades" involved in both selling and production.

Research Techniques

The major techniques adopted in market research have already been hinted at but in order to appreciate what is involved and what skills are required it is necessary to look at them in a little more detail. As with all other types of research, market research exercises revolve around the collection of information, interpretation of the findings, in order to provide a solution to the problem that has been posed, and a clear presentation of the results both in writing and orally. The ideal researcher is therefore perceptive, investigative and capable of concise, clear, written communications. He also needs to be sufficiently extrovert to present findings persuasively to management.

What goes into a typical market research survey? In other words what does a market research executive actually do? A typical *ad hoc* survey will make use of the following research inputs:

Desk Research to discover what has already been published on the subject and to provide the information needed for sampling.
Field Research among a representative sample of customers and other participants in the market, by means of personal interviews, telephone interviews, mailed questionnaires or diaries to collect original data.
Analysis of the findings using computer or hand analysis techniques.
Writing of the final report.
Oral Presentation of results.

The research executive may divide his time between the actual performance of some of the research inputs and the management of others. The largest management task in most surveys is that of the field interviewers who are responsible for the collection of the original data.

Continuous surveys make use of the same basic techniques but apply them on a larger scale.

It is evident therefore that surveys are produced not by a single person but by a team often comprising a range of skills and abilities. The research executive may well be the king-pin but he requires the supporting services of a number of others of varying disciplines and skills. In any research department you may find:

statisticians
programmers and data processing experts
field controllers
field interviewers
coding and editing clerks
graphics and production personnel.

Each has an important role to play in the final result emerging from a survey exercise.

How is Research Organized?

A further aid to deciding on the scope and nature of career opportunities in market research is some knowledge on how the research business is organized. In other words, who are the potential employers?

Market research may be carried out either by individuals working on their own or by multi-disciplinary and multi-skilled teams organized into sections or departments. Obviously the size of the market research unit will depend on the volume of work to be carried out. In general such units of varying sizes are to be found in the following environments:

Individual companies as part of the marketing department
Government departments
University marketing and business schools
Advertising agencies
Market research companies, which may in turn be:

general market research agencies offering a range of services;
specialist agencies concentrating on one of the special sub-groups of the business identified at the beginning of this chapter;
field only agencies, supplying fieldwork to other market research organizations;
market research services, such as data processing.

The principal users of market research are those organizations that have a product to sell or a service to offer, but the Government and various other institutions also make extensive use of research. Research users may carry out research for themselves or commission it from the remainder of the business. Advertising agencies and market research specialists are service organizations who carry out research on a contract basis for the research users.

The Organization of a Research Unit

Let us now consider the composition of a typical research unit. In order to indicate all the possibilities a sizeable unit is examined but in practice much smaller units with limited numbers of employees exist, in which many of the job functions are combined.

A market research company is normally run by a group of Directors. The equivalent "in-house" unit will be run by a market research manager or marketing services manager. The role of the senior individual(s) will be to convert a marketing problem into a researchable proposition. This involves specifying the information that should be obtained and the research methods that should be employed. In doing this research managers must take account not only of the ease or difficulty in obtaining specific information but also the cost of implementing the techniques proposed. The data yield should have a value which is not exceeded by the cost of collection. It is clear that a research manager or the Director of a research company must himself have considerable practical research knowledge and it is quite normal for him to have worked his way up through the research ranks.

Underneath the management level come the research executives. These may be classified into senior executives, executives, and research assistants, depending on seniority and experience. Research executives, with varying degrees of assistance and supervision, are responsible for the implementation of the research methodology, the preparation of conclusions and the presentation of findings. They can expect to face their client departments or companies in conjunction with their managers in order to account for the work they have carried out. Research is a business which inevitably gives early responsibility to staff largely because, however junior, the research executive who has directly or indirectly confronted customers is in a unique position to answer detailed questions. Senior executives will tend to be responsible for the more complex assignments and for the supervision of junior executives. Research assistants will tend to work on parts of assignments under the supervision of research executives.

The primary input to most surveys is a programme of interviews and to carry them out most research departments will have access to an interviewer field force, either directly or through an outside specialist. In consumer research where each survey may require many thousands of interviews, a large and well-managed field force is essential. In some branches of industrial research executives may be able to carry out all their own interviews but even in this more specialized sector of the research business, field forces of interviewers are becoming common. It is rare for an internal research department within a company to operate its own field force; the costs are too high relative to the use it would get. It is normal for such departments to buy-out their field requirements. A field force or field department will be administered by a field manager who is responsible for the recruitment of interviewers, the allocation of interviews to interviewers and the collection of the results. To help her (field managers are usually, though not necessarily, women) she will have field supervisors who are regionally based and look after the management of assignments on the ground, and the interviewers themselves, who will be responsible for contacting respondents according to the instructions set down by the research executives, conducting the interview and despatching the results to the research office. In continuous research operations the interviewers may work to rigid, prescribed work patterns but in *ad hoc* research they will have to exercise considerable discretion on how they carry out their tasks.

Another important service function within the research operation is the statistical department. Sample surveys rely heavily on statistical expertise in order to ensure that the sample is truly representative of the universe as a whole and that the findings can, if necessary, be grossed up to national or regional estimates. The statisticians may work in close touch with the data processing experts who, in the case of large sample surveys, will be responsible for the analysis of the returned interviews. The size and scope of the data processing function will depend on the type and scale of research being carried out. A large panel operator will be heavily dependent on his data processing not only for the accuracy of the results but also for the maintenance of tight delivery schedules. A small *ad hoc* research unit would tend to buy-out its data processing requirements from specialists.

The support of a well-stocked library containing basic information sources, statistics, directories and the results of previous research assignments, is a common prerequisite for good research and its usefulness is enhanced if it is run by an efficient information officer. The information officer can be a specialist research executive providing information for proposal writing as well as during the conduct of the surveys.

Finally, many research units will have a strong graphics and report production unit. To carry conviction it is essential that surveys are well presented as well as being well written. This means a liberal use of diagramatic presentations, in order to assist rapid assimilation of the results by busy management, and well printed reports. As far as a specialist research company is concerned, the final report is in effect their product and it is imperative that the production standards for the report enhance the general quality of the survey findings themselves.

Full Time and Part Time

One difference between market research and other marketing activities is the great propensity to use part-time and consultant staff. Interviewers, various clerical grades and even the research executives themselves may be employed on a freelance basis. The reason for this lies in the wide variations in the daily and weekly workload either centrally or in the various regions in which research is being conducted. There are therefore considerable opportunities for those whose circumstances do not permit them to undertake full-time employment or who wish to be their own masters and have greater control over when and where they wish to work. The disadvantage of the part-time role is that work cannot and will not be guaranteed all the time though freelance staff may maintain an even workload by hiring themselves to more than one research organization.

How is Research Financed?

The continued demand for market research personnel depends on the willingness of organizations to spend the required resources on such services. Funds for research have come from increasingly diverse sources in recent years, not all of which are directly involved in the marketing process. These include:

individual companies
trade associations
central and local government
financial and other institutions
political parties.

In fact it is the very diversity of research sponsors that has contributed to the wide variety of research types referred to above.

Ad hoc research contracts are, as the name implies, funded on a contract-by-contract basis. The volume of such work commissioned is dependent on business performance and confidence and a feature of the *ad hoc* research business is the cyclical demand for such services. The resultant ebb and flow in research contracts has obvious implications for employment in the business. To mitigate the effects, most large research companies seek some longer term control over their income either by asking their clients to sign long-term contracts, as is the case with continuous operations, or be embarking on study programmes which are syndicated among groups of clients.

Qualifications Required for a Career in Market Research

Graduate Staff

As one of the more academic branches of the marketing business, market research has a strong predilection for the employment of graduates for research assistant positions and above. Having said that it is also true that any intelligent person with the required data collection, interpretive, and communication skills can make a career in the business. The principal reason for employing graduates is that in obtaining their degree they have demonstrated their ability to assimilate information and produce structured answers to problems. It is therefore this aspect of the graduate's training which makes him attractive to the market research employer, rather than the specific course he has studied. Obviously graduates in the social sciences will be more drawn to market research than those in the physical sciences but from the employer's viewpoint a mechanical, electrical or electronic engineer may be just as acceptable as an economist, sociologist or psychologist, particularly if the field of study is industrial rather than consumer products.

Market research is an attractive career for those who wish to exercise communication skills but still remain within the confines of a structured discipline. As already indicated, a competent market research executive needs to be unique – a combination of the introvert and the extrovert. He needs to adopt a studied approach to the problem and make disciplined use of the various research techniques but at the same time he has to be able to express his findings clearly and persuasively. Presentations are often verbal *tours de force* during which the research executive demonstrates his complete mastery of the problem and actively promotes the marketing solution determined by the research. In the *ad hoc* research company and also in the internal research department the senior research executive must also develop into a salesman, promoting research services and converting client problems into research proposals. He will be increasingly involved in costing research assignments and convincing clients that the sums involved are worth paying.

Other Qualifications

Market research departments can absorb non-graduate qualifications such as HND or Diplomas in marketing, particularly if the course includes a strong component of statistics or survey techniques. The principal disciplines required are however within the service functions such as statisticians or computer programmers.

The large panel and retail audit companies have a substantial need for managers to run the divisionalized organization they have developed. Management will involve the motivation and direction of teams of skilled and unskilled personnel. They also have a need for client service executives. These are specialist salesmen adapting the data collected by the company to potential client requirements.

Untrained Personnel

Among the multiple tasks to be undertaken within a research unit there are a large number of opportunities for untrained staff, or at least for staff who can be trained quickly in a particular function. Many of the tasks require only native wit and intelligence to perform well. These categories include:

field interviewers
coders and editors
clerks.

The training received in these tasks may lead to promotion to supervisor or management grades within the large companies.

Market research, like many marketing functions, is labour intensive. The volume and quality of research output is dependent entirely on the number and calibre of the personnel employed. There is, of course, some opportunity to mechanize, for example in data processing, but in the main people are still the principal resource. The intake of personnel into research departments may be either direct from university or from the ranks of those that have had experience in some other marketing function. Smaller numbers of staff are recruited among school leavers, though a limited number of training posts may exist in some research operations.

Career Prospects

The career prospects within a research unit have been described in some detail in the above paragraphs, but the span from research assistant to senior research executive or even market research manager may be as little as five years. Thus a new graduate joining a research company may have effectively reached the top of the research scale by his late twenties.

Where next? for the number of directors' posts in the research business are necessarily few. In fact, the answer is simple. Market research is commonly thought to provide among the best general training in marketing, and market research personnel are greatly sought after for line jobs elsewhere within the marketing function. Research provides a view of business which is unique. It is practical in that the researcher has first-hand contact with customers and their requirements and problems: but at the same time, he obtains a strategic view of what should be done in marketing terms in order to succeed in the business. This experience will stand him in good stead in a line function.

For those who wish to remain within the research environment it is possible to progress in terms of responsibility and income either by developing specialist research skills or by moving into management roles within the bigger research companies. For the more entrepreneurial it is also practical to think in terms of forming one's own organization.

Research is an exciting start to a marketing career and for many, offers a lifelong involvement in the solution of marketing problems. For those with the necessary skills a decision to enter the research business will never be regretted.

Training in Marketing Research

Market research is now included in many of the general graduate and post-graduate degree courses. It is also covered by polytechnics and business schools and for those who wish to absorb the theory during a formal studies programme there should be no problem. Courses and seminars on market research are also available at the College of Marketing and from private seminar and conference organizations, though the frequency and content will vary from year to year.

The best advice to a would-be market researcher is to gain a good degree or basic qualification in a subject you enjoy. Direct relevance to marketing or research is not essential. The analytical skills acquired are far more important than knowledge of the subject. Training in research techniques and their application is offered by all companies that employ new graduates and will be an essential part of the first few months' employment whatever formal studies have been undertaken. Most practising market researchers know that they have learnt their most valuable lessons while actually working on assignments.

Further Information

The two professional associations within the market research business are:

The Market Research Society
175 Oxford Street
London W1R 1TA

and:

The Industrial Market Research Association
11 Bird Street
Lichfield
Staffs WS13 6PW

Both organizations publish membership lists, and the *Market Research Society Handbook* and the *International Directory of Market Research Organizations* list the market research agencies. Combined, these sources will tell you who to apply to for executive and other appointments. Research executive appointments are normally advertised in such journals as:

Campaign
The Economist
The Daily Telegraph
The Observer.

Job vacancies are also circulated by IMRA or announced in the MRS Newsletter. Research companies employing new graduates (and not all of them do) normally advise University Appointments Boards and insert details in such job directories as "Forward Vacancies".

8. Public Relations

Roger Hayes

Ask public relations recruits why they think they're God's gift to the industry and they invariably refer to their unique ability to "get on with people". True, it would be a hardship not to possess that not-so-unique ability. It is a truism to say that public relations is a people business. But it takes a certain combination of talent, experience, temperament, as well as personality to make it in this changing and growing field.

As the bridge between the organization – whether Company (private or public, capital goods or consumer), Association, Institution, Government Department, Charity or Pressure Group – and a whole range of "publics" whom that organization wishes to influence or is influenced by, the PR executive shoulders a heavy burden. He or she is not only the eyes of the organization but the mouthpiece too. In short PR requires people who are interested in talking to anyone and who demonstrably, either through academic attainment or experience – preferably both – has a feel for "what makes people tick" and the various skills needed to inform and persuade.

A well known manual on public relations states the requirements for the job: "They must be sufficiently articulate in speech and on paper to explain policies, plans, achievements and events in a way that commands attention. They must have creative imagination and a streak of opportunism, tempered by a balanced judgement. They must be good managers, of money and time and be able to work under pressure. They must possess complete integrity." To these personal qualities and fundamental communications abilities should be added academic or practical experience in any or all (perhaps not quite all) of a wide range of disciplines: marketing, home economics, personnel management, market research, social psychology, the law, journalism, history, literature, politics and international relations. All can be valuable skills in an increasingly sophisticated environment.

If you still think you are suited to public relations and can cope with anything from the writing of articles, speeches, annual reports and brochures to putting together audio-visual aids and making presentations, then read on.

Public relations is not a suspect, fringe activity, a cosmetic without foundation. It is a crucial function in a world that is increasingly complex, critical, organized and articulate, that wants to know what is produced, how things are run, what the implications are, and who is responsible. It is up to organizations, whatever shape or size and position in society, to be responsive to changing expectations. Consumers, bankers, shareholders, politicians, doctors, trade unionists and other specialist groups are the market place of the PR executive or public relations officer. They are the "publics" that may have to be reached with a carefully tailored message.

The traditional "publics" of companies are shareholders and customers. But as our organization adapts to change it must treat with equal concern the newer "stakeholders" — employees who demand a greater share in the wealth and decision-making process, for example and government who restrict and legislate in the "public interest". Companies and government departments are having to cope with a growing band of articulate and organized minorities – pressure groups who demand that their case be heard. If you work for a pressure group, politicians along with the media will be one of your prime targets.

Let's have a look then at the overall public relations function, in one of its most familiar contexts, the promotion of "goods and services". The trouble is that it is a technique which covers virtually every part of communications except that which involves buying space, which is the province of the advertising people. Even this function is often part of public relations, e.g. corporate advertising. You can't simply say "we need more PR" – as someone did at a recent sales conference when he actually wanted more money to be spent on tombola prizes for his buyer's benevolent society dances – because public relations is about total communications. It is not only about reaching your customer with the message that will linger on, but it is also about reaching his customers too.

The essence of good public relations is planning. To be effective public relations cannot be *ad hoc*. It starts with long hours studying market research results, psychological surveys and salesmen's reports so that at the end of the day we have an indentikit picture in our mind of the particular customer and the influences that motivate him. Is it his wife? Then let's go for coverage in the women's magazines or sponsor a women's golf tournament. Is it his colleagues? Then we will need spots at trade conferences, exhibitions, training sessions and management courses. Is it his trade magazines? Then we will have to give them some hard news stories and feature articles that will generate a sense of authority and sales potential in the twenty or thirty trade magazines that will possibly impinge on his life. In nine cases out of ten all these factors are already influencing his thinking before you even arrive on the scene. More important, he's thinking all the time about whether or not the customers that come into his store or respond to his mail order catalogue will actually make the purchase. This is where we move into the more sophisticated areas because we're not simply trying to reach his customers head-on through a mention in the Sunday papers or a compliment in a consumer column in one of the tabloids, but we aim to create a total climate of opinion where all the potential customer's friends and acquaintances also discuss and know all about the product or service in question.

In the area of food and drink products, customers turn to a hundred and one different sources and authorities for their opinions. It may be from the idle reading of some "pop" nutritional article in a Sunday colour magazine; this will mean we have to ensure that as high a proportion as possible of likely writers on the subject know the hard nutritional facts about your product. It could be the domestic science teacher at school who first helped form their attitudes, in which case a highly organized, carefully planned series of "soft-sell" seminars at teacher training colleges may be the answer. Or it could be the health visitor, the nurse, the local GP or the gym coach at the health club who first provided the germ of an idea which later hardened into an opinion.

It does not matter whether you are selling food and drink items or more "considered-purchase" products like cars and computers, the fact remains that customers are motivated by hundreds of outside influences and the customer's customers by even more such stimuli.

The role of public relations is to try and isolate as many sectors of this complex decision-making process as possible. Having done that, we have to slice those customers up psychologically, socially and economically. As you can see the job of public relations entails more than information and promotion, it also has to do with understanding and acceptance.

It is important to realize that the techniques of communicating a message effectively require all the ingredients, not just some of them. The role of public relations in this marketing mix is only just beginning to be accepted. There really is no point in devoting £500,000 to an advertising budget and then wondering why the PR gives so few results on a budget of £10,000. Most public relations effort comes from the man - or woman-hours put into it and this is where the money should be placed.

Public relations has a different marketing job to that of advertising. Whereas advertising (subject to certain legal and voluntary controls) allows you to say what you like, where you like, public relations does none of these things. What it does is to allow you to extend the corporate or sales message in more depth. The advertising copywriter must get it all into one headline and twenty words of bodycopy. Public relations aims to persuade a journalist to write a 1,000-word feature article, a lecturer to talk about the subject in his lectures or a home economics teacher to use the product in the class-room. If your message is a complex one, then an in-depth interview leading to a radio programme or a good news story in *The Times* is the ideal way to get it across.

Editorial coverage must be a useful adjunct to advertising. We know from research that consumers are more likely to notice a message and to react favourably to it if they receive it through a number of different channels rather than being pummelled through direct advertising alone.

So, public relations allows you to extend your message, use a wider range of communication channels, and because other people are involved in carrying the message for you, such as journalists, teachers, or opinion formers, there is the advantage that comes from a third party endorsement. How much more effective it is when a girl says "I've heard such marvellous things about you. I've always wanted to meet you" than for you to tell her how marvellous you are! That is the difference between public relations and salesmanship.

The companies which are using public relations in a truly effective way are the successful companies, the ones with the high-calibre management and the funds to test their decisions through market research. Although it is difficult to prove the effectiveness of the public relations function in the way you can prove a salesman's efficiency, all the signs show that products move more quickly off the shelf when marketing, advertising and public relations all move in step with the salesman's personal efforts.

But if the area of marketing PR is one of the least understood it is certainly where it all began – with the placement of editorial coverage. Whilst customers may still be the most important audience, without whom a company ceases to exist, public relations in the last decade has poked its nose into every facet of modern business life.

First it was the financial world. The City of London, ever ready to react to change, realized that hiding one's good work under a bushel was "not on". In a brand new world of tabloid "city pages" with everyone having a flutter on the stock exchange (thanks to unit trusts), it had to climb down from its splendid isolation. The fortress around the City's square mile remained but the drawbridge was opened so that the City could explain its inner workings. Perhaps that is why the City is as powerful and successful as it is. It recognizes new thinking when an idea is still only a twinkle in the eye of the rest of the world.

Equally, publicly-quoted companies soon began to realize that it was not only Aunt Fanny in Devon who had a couple of hundred shares that they had to keep in touch with, and then only once a year, but the far more powerful city institutions. Now there are year-round programmes aimed at a variety of City audiences, ranging from the banks and pension funds to stockbrokers.

Soon afterwards public relations moved into the corridors of governmental power. There had always been the few specialized big accounts, the governmental campaigns of the 50s. Roy Welensky's Central African Federation, the East German Trade account and the Angola affair, made and almost broke one or two "name" consultancies during that period. Apart from a few small operations doing little more than a parliamentary monitoring service, few corporations at that time were engaged in properly planned campaigns over a number of years aimed to change legislation or create a "dialogue" with official and public opinion. This has all changed now and many PR people see it as the growth area of the 1980s.

The next area of expansion was corporate public relations. Paradoxically, universal education forced this new thinking upon company management. The 1944 Education Act made revolutionaries of us all. It taught every pressure group from the Friends of the Earth to the Housewives Trust how to use the media and lean on government, both local and national, in order to achieve change. Suddenly companies found themselves under pressure. Five well-educated hippies with an axe to grind could mobilize a community to oppose a new oil refinery, demand drastic alterations to the labelling of a supermarket product or simply cause a kink in a roadway plan.

From the world of public affairs – as we rather grandly call it – it was but a short step into the sacred board-room itself. There, public relations became part of corporate life, however grudgingly the marriage was consummated. No longer could the financial director calmly publish his yearly figures, complete with soporifics from the Chairman, to an apathetic share-holding community. Now he had to consider the impact it might have on labour relations. Consumerist shareholders were even beginning to ask probing questions at the AGM. Senior management realized that the messages aimed at these audiences had to be consistent, whatever was being said, whenever it was being said. In the age of the "global village", it is no good telling a financial audience in London that profits are up if you have just told workers in Milan they can't have a rise. News travels faster now than it did in the days of Julius Reuter's pigeon courier.

Public relations then, had arrived in the board-room. No longer was it simply a technique for communicating messages, it was the message itself. If the product wasn't right the public relations would not work either. You couldn't put white-wash over dry rot, at least not for long. The successful company slowly but surely began to involve public relations in the very process of corporate thinking, until it has now become integral to the decision-making process.

Woe betide the company that pollutes a river or soils the linen on the washing line. Short-sighted corporate decisions, combined with superficial or non-existent public relations, can affect the very survival of a company.

Ironically, the more we move into the twenty-first century with electronic gadgets to ease our path to better communication, whether by the use of electronic news gathering (ENG) or the home television screen to provide instant data on everything from cricket scores to stock market prices (e.g. CEEFAX, ORACLE, PRESTEL), the more use we make of audio-visual aids, ultimately we come down to face-to-face communication as the key to success. Nowhere is this more true than in the growing area of internal communications.

After all, it is employees that are the company and without them no products would be produced. Historically the public relations business has concentrated on external relations, but so often if you don't keep your own house in order it won't matter how well you promote yourselves externally. An undermotivated workforce whose morale is sapped will not produce sufficient product of high enough standard to satisfy customer demand. The company will gain a reputation in the local community as a bad employer, which impedes recruitment. If it is a large employer in that community it will incur the wrath of the local politicians and newspapers not to mention the trade unions. Shareholders may well become jittery and the share price fall below its real value. Government may step in; the company will be the subject of headlines it cannot control and which are bound to give an unbalanced view. A host of unsatisfied customers will by now have switched their allegiance to a competitor. It is a tough world in which the role of public relations is increasingly being recognized.

In the current industrial relations climate, the ability to communicate management policies and involve employees in the evolution of the company is one of the crucial aspects of public relations. The tendency towards large units both in industry and central/local government has increased the need to interpret decisions and skilfully to those who must implement and live with them. Good house journals, briefing groups, closed circuit television, features, an employee annual report, all help to counter rumour and hearsay with facts and information. If management and employees have always shared a trusting relationship, then if bad times come and the plant is forced to make people redundant, the exercise is handled with the minimum of misunderstanding. Legislation has certainly speeded up the process towards greater disclosure of information and consultation with employees and unions.

Like financial or employee relations, the world of government and politics is another specialist area for public relations people. A carefully planned programme is required, directing messages to selected politicians so as to build up a nucleus of support for your case, whether it be to initiate, change or just modify legislation. This can take the form of background briefings with MPs, the mailing of literature to those who have knowledge of or interest in the subject, a letter to *The Times* or the tabling of a parliamentary question which gains publicity for an issue generating interest amongst the public at large, who in turn exercise their influence at the ballot box. It could equally well be a series of meetings with EEC Commissioners who like to be consulted before policy decisions are made or initiating a debate in the European Parliament.

Legislation is encroaching on industry in a wide variety of areas from packaging and labelling to company law. Organizations are no longer free to do as they please and consequently need to make their voices heard in Whitehall and Westminster, not to mention Brussels and Strasbourg, if they are not to be victims of legislation, regulations or directives emanating from the corridors of power.

Although politicians and civil servants may be the focus of any public affairs campaign they are influenced by and in turn influence the media and public opinion. So that messages directed at different levels via a variety of channels have a cumulative effect leading hopefully to a change in government policy towards the building of a new motorway or technical changes to a new Bill passing through Parliament.

Because businesses are becoming more and more vulnerable, especially those where the hazards of fire or pollution are great, public relations increasingly has a role in training managements to deal with irritable local councillors, persistent journalists, sceptical customers, cynical salesmen, and ivory tower ecologists. Seminars are run by public relations people for company executives undertaking role-playing exercises. For a day they are taught to make speeches, handle actors who have been well rehearsed, appear on television and deal with a major disaster situation, such as an oil-rig fire, all in life-like conditions.

Public relations is now moving into even higher gear, not simply projecting the corporate image but also examining how the organization should fulfil its role in society beyond its primary one, the creation of wealth. This wider concept is embraced by that much-abused phrase "social responsibility", and the method for measuring it, the "social audit".

The terms "social responsibility" and "social audit" are understood across frontiers, even if they are abused by some and misunderstood by others. Social accountability, the responsibilities of business, the unacceptable face of capitalism, industrial democracy, the rights of minorities – these and many other expressions have become buzz words, in phrases used widely in speeches by businessmen and politicians and even public relations people when looking for evidence of change.

There is a growing awareness within our institutions that a *response* is needed, not just to criticism, some of which is ill-founded and inaccurate, but also to the genuine demands of a rapidly changing social, political and economic environment.

So we are no longer talking about *why* social responsibility is necessary, but about *how business should adapt to societal changes*. In other words, social responsibility is integral to and not separate from a company's function of producing and making profit. Social responsibility is no longer an optional extra. It is ultimately about survival, and the lessons for public relations executives, acting as the corporate monitor, conscience, early-warner and communicator are obvious. It is our job to reflect the character of a company and, by monitoring, reflect the view of its many publics, then develop programmes to satisfy them. Although I have been writing about companies to explain the changing nature of this fascinating business, the principles remain the same whatever organization you are working for.

If public relations seems a vague and amorphous term it is probably not only because it has to encompass such a range of activities, but also because it is used by such a variety of employers. Listed below are the main categories of employers of public relations specialists.

Central Government

Each government department has its own information staff. As well as advising ministers and officials on the department's public relations, such staff deal directly with the press, the BBC and Independent Television, radio and newsreel companies, in many aspects of their work. There is also the Central Office of Information (COI) which acts as a common service agency for all government departments for the preparation, supply and often distribution of publicity material, of reference material required for use both at home and overseas, and of technical advice and assistance on publicity matters. COI is also one of the biggest advertisers in the country and this demonstrates the frequent overlapping of these two functions.

Local Government

Since the creation of the new authorities there has been an expansion of the use of public relations personnel in local government, health and water services. The Police and the Fire Brigade also employ PR personnel.

Nationalized Industries

The electricity boards, gas boards, publicly owned airlines and other state-owned operations are substantial employers of public relations officers either under that name or as press and information officers.

Financial Institutions & The City

Financial institutions such as insurance companies, banks and merchant banks use public relations to market their services and to communicate their performance to the public, shareholders, or political parties. PR is also vital in such matters as takeover battles, mergers or launching a new share issue. Such institutions may use their own PR people or employ a consultancy. City groups such as the British Insurance Association, the Accepting House Committee or banking information services are now organized to provide information officers. The City is also involved with international aspects of PR. There is even a City Communications Organization (CCO) whose difficult task is to act as clearing house and contact point for the media in dealing with city institutions.

Professional, Trade, Social & Voluntary Organizations

PR departments in this field vary in size and scope as they do in private industry. Employers include such bodies as trade unions, trade associations, professional institutes, charities and educational establishments.

Public Relations Consultancies

These may be independent or associated with an advertising agency. They may be large or small, specialize in a particular field such as Public Affairs or financial work, or may offer a total package of PR services. A consultancy acquires clients and details a senior person to manage and organize their accounts. He or she will be assisted by a team which spends either all or part of its time working on the client's behalf.

There is much scope in local government which should increase with the trend towards devolution and greater community involvement. The PR departments of the nationalized industries vary in size from one man to huge staffs. They have a commercial flavour as well as a good deal of political accountability, which must be reflected in public relations activity. There are a variety of PR openings in professional institutes, fund-raising charities, educational establishments, trade associations and trade unions. The City's complex nexus of insurance companies, banks, broking houses and associations and organizations representing different facets of "the square mile" all have PROs or a consultancy representing them. Any such list of possible employers does not include the growing number of opportunities in international organizations and UK or international companies at marketing/corporate level.

On any given day, the PR executive may be attending to the detailed logistics of a major plant opening, sponsoring a sporting or cultural event, undertaking a market survey, running an air race to promote a product, working with MPs to modify legislation, writing an employee version of the annual report, trying to stop an oil refinery being built in a residential local community, raising funds for a newly independent school, developing a new corporate indentity from a mish-mash of subsidiary company names and symbols, training the chairman to appear on TV, working alongside bankers and lawyers on the tactics of a take-over bid, or explaining an increase in gas prices or a new government measure to journalists.

Before getting into PR you need a great deal of imagination to predict all the activities with which you might become involved.

Of course, it all depends on your special skills and in which part of the PR world you end up.

PR has been said to improve everyone's image but its own. It has been criticized in the past by those in professions on whose territory it encroaches; accountants, lawyers, bankers and personnel officers, by politicians who are the foremost practitioners of the art but would abhor the description, and by journalists with whom PR has long shared as ambivalent but interdependent relationship.

One of the frustrations of public relations is that it defies definition in a strict sense and people have different expectations of what it can do. It is therefore difficult to marry up precisely your talents and interests to a public relations job. Its joy, however, is that once you have found your niche it stretches you to the limit and you know you are a pioneer in a rapidly growing field. The more techniques are used to evaluate our effectiveness, the more our customers are convinced it is a job well done, and the higher salaries will rise. It is a function of demand and supply. The key element will be to find the right quality of executive.

Whilst our image remains important the related matter of status will become increasingly so. And that will depend on attracting, motivating and training some of the best young talent around. But if you still think, having read the chapter, that PR is a combination of whitewash and smooth talk epitomized by the man in the pin striped suit wining and dining someone else's money away at a West End Club, don't bother to knock on any PR doors. We would be polite but firm and send you back to check up on your facts. We may be in the people business but we are also in the facts business. Although we would be glad to inform you that you have got the job in public relations it is first up to you to persuade us to give you the job.

9. A PRACTICAL COURSE OF ACTION

Roderick Braithwaite

Now that you've read through this far, well done! At least you've got part of that essential ingredient for a career in the world of communications and marketing – stamina and preserverance.

Alternatively you may also have part of another of those essential ingredients – opportunism, and you may have jumped straight to Chapter 9. Well I'm sorry to disappoint you opportunists for the moment, but you'll get more out of this chapter by returning to Go, i.e. to the Introduction and then to Chapter 1.

The age, sex, nationality and previous qualifications of those who read this book are clearly widely different. So the practical advice will need to vary too.

However, summing up, a little lightly, the previous chapters, if this chapter is to be of any use to you, you will need to possess a good sprinkling of the following characteristics, which I will call here "the desirable dozen": see Figure 9.1.

All right so far? You see yourself in this amalgam, do you? Fine. Read on!

Am I the Right Kind of Person? What's the Evidence?

Don't get this wrong. Clearly, in this highly diverse world of ours, there is room for a wide variety of talents, ambitions, qualifications, and you certainly don't need one hundred per cent of each element in that desirable dozen to play a part in the world of communications. However you do need a pretty high quota of each of those characteristics to stay the course right through your career, and to succeed. So ponder very hard at the outset as to whether you think you've got what it takes. Look objectively at all the things you've done up to now, at school, out of school, at

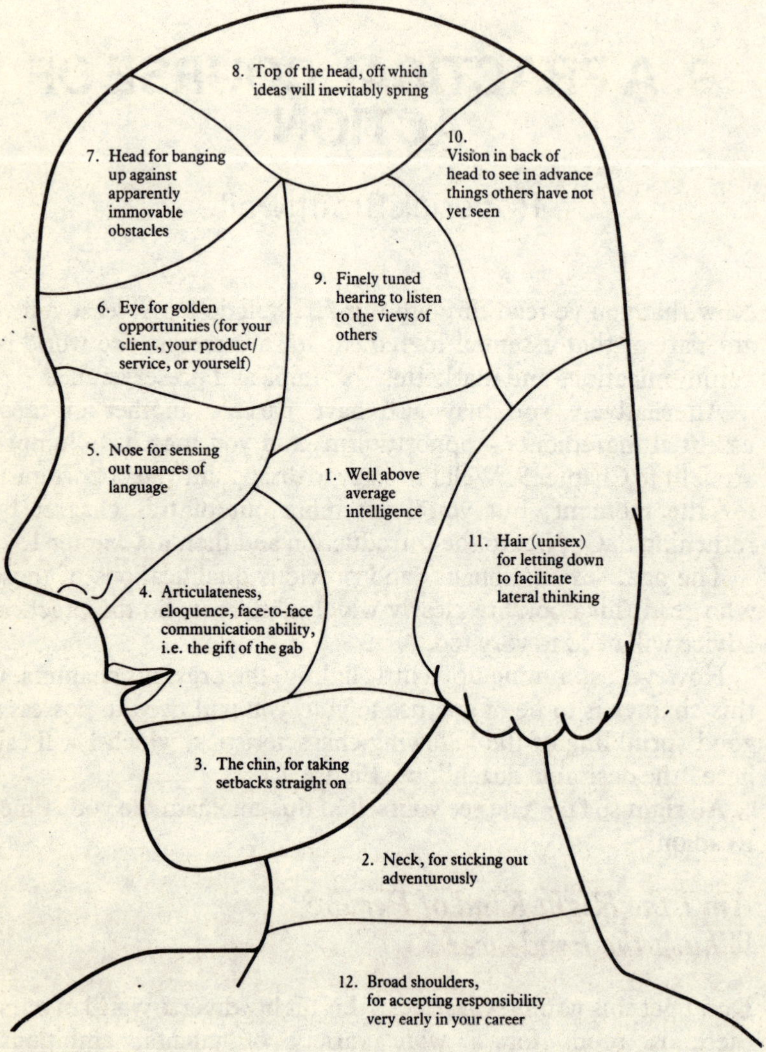

Figure 9.1

university, or in any jobs or tasks you have had the good fortune to tackle. You've got to ask yourself at least the following seven questions:

1 Am I the sort of person who wants to change things?
2 Can I influence those around me?
3 Do I like talking to others?
4 Do I get on well with people?
5 Have I got the patience to persuade and convince?
6 Do other people interest me?
7 Do I manage to keep bouncing back even when things seem to be against me?

(To these might also be added the ability to analyse problems, and to organize and control the solutions to such problems.)

Am I, in other words, sufficient of an extrovert to make this kind of career a starter in my own personal career race?

The Formal or the Informal Route?

Let us assume that you have satisfied yourself on this preliminary hurdle in that race. The next question is: What can I do to get started?

Here you might see yourself as a canoeist, alone, with a couple of paddles, amidst the broad waters of what I hope by now you've accepted as being a very fast-moving, unpredictable river, which can quite easily engulf the unprepared, the unskilful, the timid, the heavy-handed or the unstable.

As a novice to this race, you have two choices. The formal route, or the informal route.

The formal route consists of spending your immediate period ahead in a study/learning phase, and for this you must take on board all the advice offered in Chapter 2. This, if you like, is the officially marked-out course, the middle of the stream, the one statistically most likely to bring you to the finishing post still intact and of sound mind. There is not much more to be said on this: it is by far the most efficient course for that fragile canoe of yours!

The informal course is away from the smoother waters, it could bring you across unsuspected currents, over shoals and rocks, crashing into the bank on either side, or even divert you completely into tributaries, so that you never get back into the mainstream of marketing and communications again. Its essence is that of getting a job *somewhere* vaguely near the mainstream, and then taking it from there.

These two routes need not, of course, be mutually exclusive, and we will look later on at a kind of composite "critical path" to see how the two routes can interact. However it is important to say that many successful people in the market place got there initially via the informal route. No doubt they were lucky, but the other half of good luck is opportunism – seeing chances when they arise. No doubt therefore that all those who followed the informal route were pre-destined by their personal qualities to arrive eventually in a job of the entrepreneurial kind represented by communications and marketing; but the secret was that they kept their antennae tuned to the opportunities that subsequently occurred, so as to actually get inside the magic circle.

Thus, as you will see in Figure 9.2, we have laid some emphasis on getting a job *somewhere*, which will at least give you a starting point, an introduction to commercial life, to working with others. It may not necessarily seem like an Open Sesame to you at the time, but if what the authors of the previous chapters have said has struck up a sufficiently vital spark of interest in your mind, then your own determination will sooner or later be able to espy the second or third job-opening which will bring that spark bursting into flame – and you will have "broken through".

Some Examples: What Can I Learn from These?

As a background to looking at Figure 9.2, just consider the following examples taken from real-life – i.e. actual people who exist at this moment – who have come in via a more or less informal route. For brevity we have kept this list down to the same level of a dozen, as those characteristics we talked about earlier.

Mr. A: entered Royal Navy as midshipman: now at 45 Chairman of a major international communications group of companies.

Miss B: left school and got job in a Fleet Street newspaper office. Now via a subsequent MBA at Cranfield, and at 29, marketing manager of a range of publications.

Mrs. C: left art school for studio designer's job in a major retail store. Now, at 40, creative director of an advertising agency.

Mr. D: went from school into banking. Now, at 40, chief executive of a financial advertising agency.

Mrs. E: left university with languages degree and taught English. Now, at 35, research consultant in a major market research company.

Miss F: left university with a degree in history, and got job first in various firms, then in The Industrial Society. Now, at 27, executive in the employee communications division of a public relations consultancy.

Mr. G: left school and trained as a mechanical engineer in industry. Now, at 43, managing director of a recruitment advertising agency.

Mr. H: left school with 2 O-levels and got series of jobs connected with retailing, starting as petrol pump attendant. Now leading copywriter in consumer advertising, at 45.

Mr. I: left school to be a salesman with a detergent and soap company. Now, at 47, runs marketing and training consultancy.

Mr. J: left school and entered Civil Service as an executive officer. Now, at 34, account supervisor in an advertising agency.

Mr. K: left school for job as retail merchandising executive. Now, at 48, chairman of an international manufacturing company.

Miss L: currently at university, having originally aimed at teaching. Now, at 22, engaged in pursuing the informal approach (see later).

On reading these brief examples, ask yourself at least these three questions:

1 Do I recognize myself in any of these?
2 Do any of those career-progressions interest me?
3 What lessons can I draw for myself from them?

In other words, as the saying goes, there are many ways of skinning the cat! If you think about *yourself* creatively, and adventurously, as all these people undoubtedly had to, then the breaks will come. However, that must sound like pie in the sky to you at this moment in your career: keep it in the back of your mind, when we analyse out how the various entry points and levels of qualification, and the formal/informal routes, can interact.

What Am I, and What Route Can I Follow?

We suggest you look carefully at Figure 9.2, relating it to the

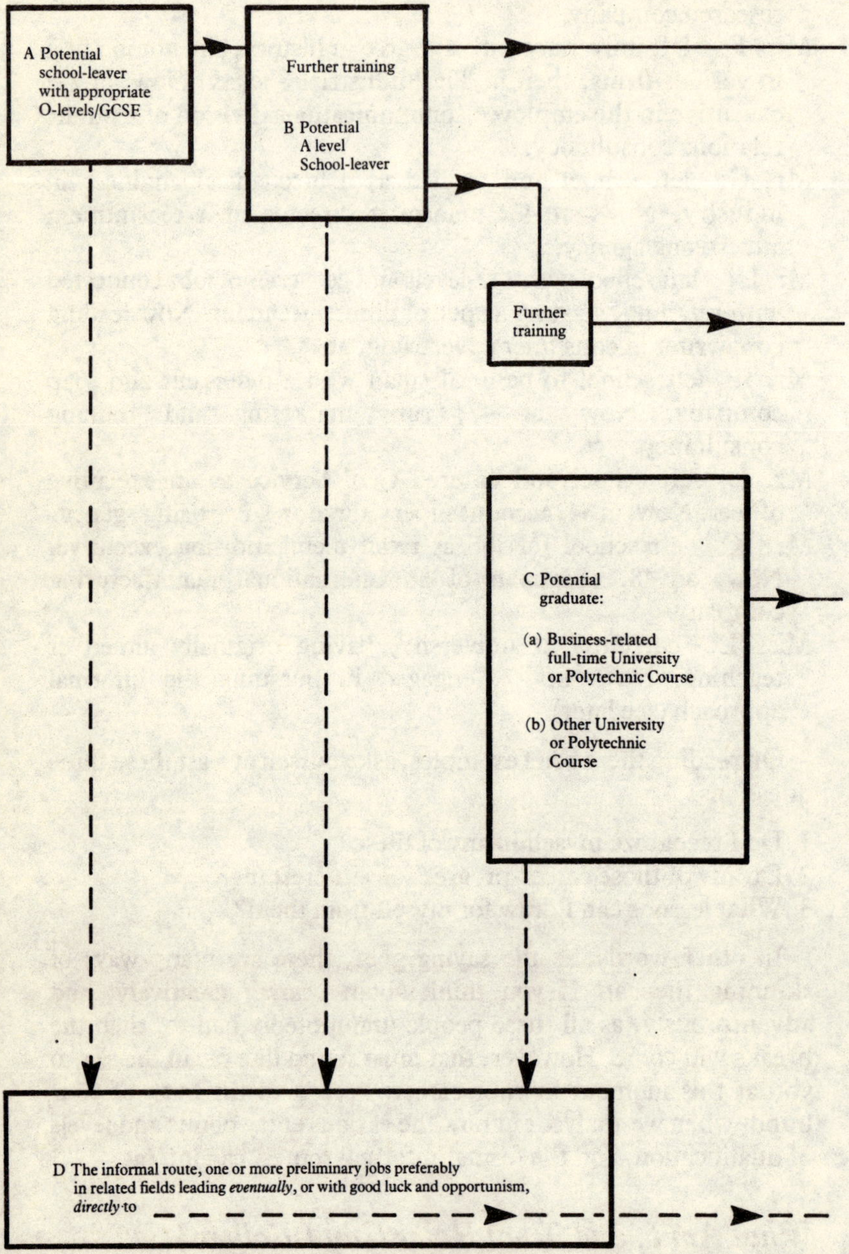

Figure 9.2 Getting in: the formal and informal routes

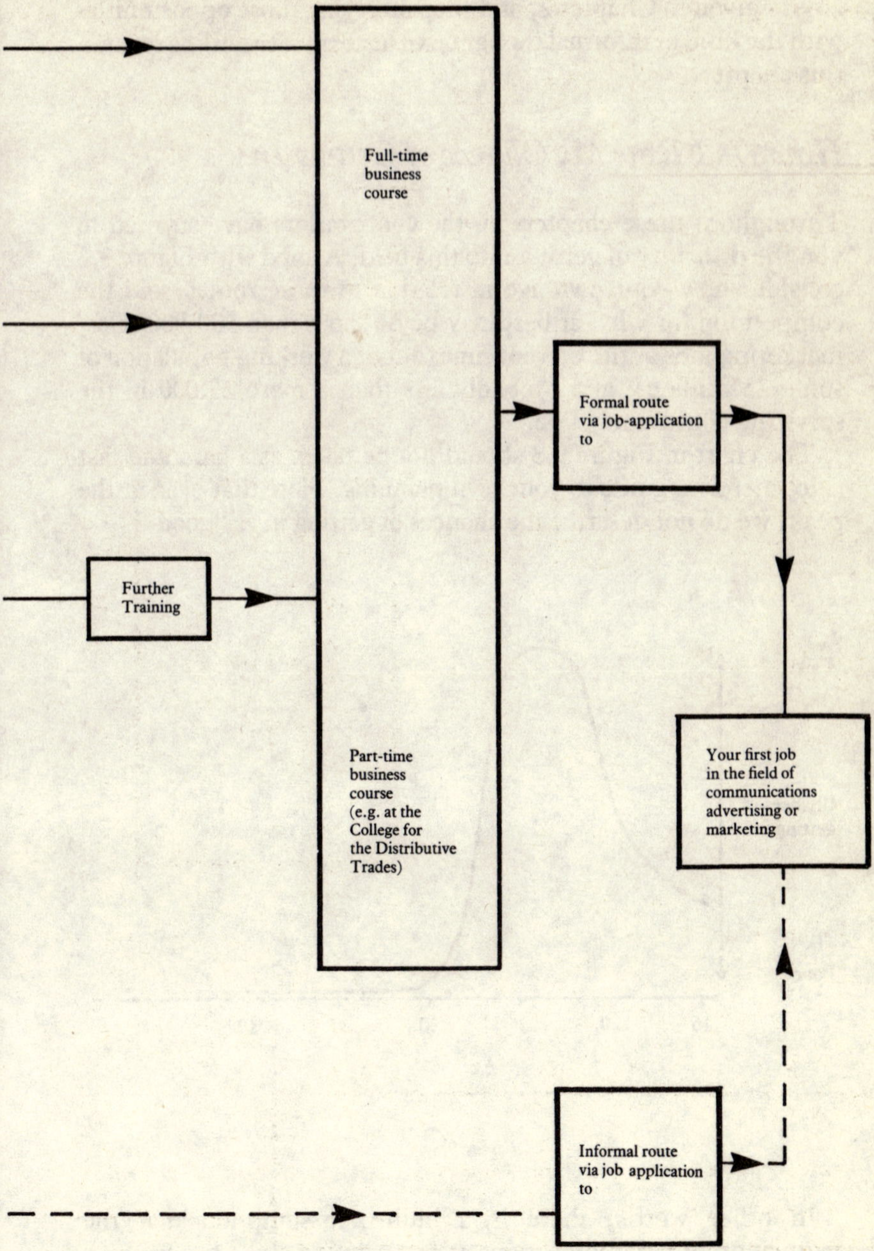
Full-time business course
Part-time business course (e.g. at the College for the Distributive Trades)
Further Training
Formal route via job-application to
Your first job in the field of communications advertising or marketing
Informal route via job application to

advice given in Chapter 2, and thus marrying those opportunities with the kind of informal thoughts we have tried to outline so far in this chapter.

How Do I Rate My Chance of Getting In?

Throughout these chapters all the contributors have stressed to you the difficulty of getting into this field. Armed with Figure 9.2 consider now your own age in relation to those routes, and the competition for what at best may be no more than 500,000 sales/marketing jobs at the present time (out of a working population of some 25 million), and probably less than a mere 25,000 in the servicing consultancy side.

The chart in Figure 9.3 should not be taken as a hard and fast rule, merely a guide to your own planning. Note that even at the peak, we do not describe the chances of getting in as "good"!

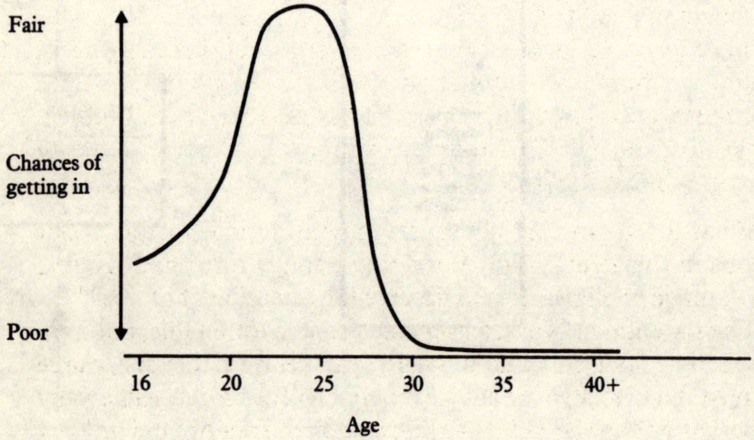

Figure 9.3

In other words, there is a built-in assumption that the acquisition of communications and marketing skills has to come early in your career, whatever your previous background and experience may have been.

At that first point in the chart however, i.e. on leaving school, don't misinterpret the nature of the opening: it may be very junior indeed, and indeed current employment legislation does not assist you by expanding that bridge-head.

Getting That First Job: How Do I Plan It?

Let's be quite clear at this stage. If you don't try hard, you won't get in at all. So you have to *want* to. Even if you try, try and try again, you still may not succeed, if you haven't got the sort of attitudes, aptitudes, presence, personality and characteristics that potential employers are looking for.

Is there a formula for success in getting that first job in the market?

Well, there is of course the whole area of interviews, and this is an aspect already so well documented that you would best be advised to study it separately: we offer a few information sources at the end of this book. Let us hope and assume you will indeed do that, so here you are starting to think in hard practical terms: how do I begin to plan it all?

There is no magic, but here are a few – another convenient dozen, as it happens – practical, horse's mouth, down-to-earth questions to ask yourself, with a view to starting the ball rolling. Hopefully, you will find these thoughts of relevance, whatever your position on Figure 9.2.

1 What more can I do to immerse myself in information about jobs in this field – is my mind well-enough furnished? Have I yet made enough effort to deserve the attention of others?
2 The parental networks: a very square suggestion this, but have I really got all the value and help I can get from that one source most likely to give me advice if only I will ask for it, namely my parent or guardian? I don't know all their friends, and unless I ask, how can I benefit from this vital source of information on my own doorstep?
3 Can I make a list of all other relatives I have who know *something* related to this field, and will they be prepared to give some advice?
4 Which of my own friends have jobs in this field, and to what extent can I trust their judgement in relation to me?

5 Who else do I know who could actually take me round such a company, simply so that I can acclimatize myself?
6 In the absence of such direct help, have I used all those advisory services available to me locally – teachers/supervisors, career guidance officers, appointments board counsellors, the Job Centre, etc.?
7 In conjunction with this, who do I know of sufficient seniority in any organization to whom I could write to ask *them* to put me in touch with *their* appropriate executive, who in turn might be prepared to see me, even if for advice only, for thirty minutes or so?
8 If I know no-one, which companies or organizations do I know something about, which at least I would like to work for, or whose products or services I find interesting, so as to give myself some kind of short-list?
9 Have I organized my exposure to the kinds of press advertising that could guide my thinking and even offer me an actual job-opportunity?
10 Am I doing this on a regular basis, not just when I feel like it, and have I worked out where I can go to see this kind of information free, e.g. local library?
11 Have I prepared a short summary about myself, my qualifications, qualities and ambitions, with the help of someone who knows about these things? Where can I get this typed and duplicated?
12 Above all, perhaps, am I starting this process early enough ahead, in relation to when I would like to start work? (Six months is probably the minimum.)

My Application: Have I Put Enough Application Behind It?

Let us assume that out of all this self-questioning and comparison-shopping between various alternatives, you find yourself with the name, title and address of the first potential employer you have yet encountered. Now comes the question of your application, and – forgive the pun – how much "application" you put into that process, how much thought, care, time, effort and subtlety.

You may recall our Miss L earlier on. She is actually currently applying to me for a job, and unknown to her, although I do not yet have a job to offer her, I am more than fifty per cent disposed to try and find something for her, or at least give her a little more of my hard-pressed executive time(!) Why is that? What is she doing so well at the point-of-sale as it were, that has helped her? Let me try to sum up the points in her favour, and I hope that these are the sort of things that any potential boss in our field would be looking for in any kind of trainee, or first-job seeker. Again, there are a dozen factors that seem to me to be worth highlighting.

1 I heard of the application through one of the established careers guidance channels, so I can assume *some* degree of pre-vetting beforehand.
2 She happens to be at a good university: but the real point is that this is simply a short-hand reassurance to me that she is intelligent, and can work hard.
3 She showed in her application form that she had already done something to develop her understanding of the communications field, through a vacation job.
4 She also showed even in her application form that she had a distinct personality and character in her own right.
5 I could read her writing, and her writing communicated to me in articulate English.
6 Although I could offer no definite job, she persisted in her correspondence with me, in the nicest firmest way, convincing me that she actually did want to work for us.
7 She turned up on time when I finally fixed an interview, even though this was at some inconvenience to herself.
8 She was cleanly and attractively dressed without overdoing it, and she had a pleasant, fresh, open outlook on life.
9 She had gone to some trouble to find out about us as an employer, and had thought through the reasons why she would like to work for us.
10 She was genuinely interested in finding out more about us.
11 She had no illusions about the relative value of her previous qualifications in straight vocational terms, and seemed prepared to do a practical job of work if we were to appoint her.
12 I judged that if we were eventually to offer her a job of some kind we would get value for money out of her, that our organization would find her compatible, and that she would have growth and development potential, without wanting to go

faster than we could cope with.

So there you have one actual employer's personal reaction to a candidate. You can see some of the factors that an employer has to have in his mind, and perhaps you can think yourself into the mind of Miss L too, to see how she managed all that! I hope she doesn't sound too much like a paragon of all the virtues, but clearly she had applied herself to the task of applying for a job and she deserves to win.

My First Job: Vantage-Point or Strait Jacket?

The essential thing to bear in mind is that your first job gives you that vital chance to get your bearings. It is the break-through out of the vicious circle of "no job therefore no expertise", "no experience therefore no job".

In that job, you can assess your new employer and the career opportunity he may offer you. You can assess your new industry, and the parts of it that relate to your job. You can begin to know which firms are good to work for, which bosses seem to run good companies, what kind of people tend to work for whom, what the trends of business are – the whole "culture" in other words. So the question answers itself: it need never be a strait jacket, limiting all your subsequent decisions and actions.

Treat it seriously, however. The marketing and communications world is quite a small parish. If you produce too many waves early on, if your new employer starts getting some uneasy vibes about you, then not surprisingly word will get along the grapevine, and you will find it less easy to move on and progress. Don't make changes in your career just for the fun of it: obviously you need from time to time to make certain moves, but don't get labelled as a hedge-hopper – they make awkward employees! Try to keep any moves you do make within some kind of overall pattern, which will make sense not only in your own terms, but also in the eyes of any subsequent employer.

Perhaps in a few years time, it will be your turn to write the updated chapter to this book itself. Let us hope that not only the advice we have all tried to give has actually been of some practical help to you, but that you have also been able to discover some of the many things that we have probably failed to cover, so that you can in turn fill in the gaps and correct the record for those who will then be looking to *you* for guidance.

Meanwhile, best wishes for your career, and above all let us hope that you enjoy it and get as much job-satisfaction from it as all of us have.

Glossary of Job Titles

Norman A. Hart

The following is a list of the most common job titles used in the fields of communication, advertising and marketing. The explanations or job descriptions given are those most frequently encountered although there are often wide deviations from these in individual organizations. It has not been practicable to allow for differences in sex, and hence the title "salesman" could equally apply to "saleswoman".

The use of certain specialized or jargon terms is inevitable and for an explanation of these, readers are referred to the *Glossary of Marketing Terms* by Norman A. Hart and John Stapleton published by Heinemann (Third edition 1987).

Account Administrator performs important specialist functions in the larger recruitment advertising agencies, part client service executive, part media buyer, acting direct to classified sales departments of media houses.

Account Director is responsible in an advertising agency for control and direction of services to a number of clients (or accounts), usually through the intermediary of a number of Account Executives.

Account Executive is concerned with the day-to-day provision of services and management of a client's requirements in an advertising agency. Sometimes known as Account Supervisor.

Advertising Manager (officer or executive) is responsible for planning and implementing his company's advertising, also for managing the advertising department. Alternatively, may be known as Publicity Manager, Sales Promotion Manager, Marketing Services Manager.

Advertisement Manager (or Director) is responsible for selling advertising on behalf of a publisher, television, radio station or display contractor. Also responsible for managing the advertisement department. Not to be confused with an Advertising Manager.

Area Sales Manager manages the sales force in a specific geographical area, and ensures an adequate level of attention to all customers and prospects in that area.

Art Director usually employed in an advertising agency or design studio, and is concerned mainly with the preparation of finished artwork from initial roughs or visuals. Such artwork may be produced in-house by staff artists, or bought out from specialist studios or freelance designers.

Brand Manager is the executive responsible for the overall marketing, and particularly promotion, of a specific brand. Job function ranges from a co-ordination role to one in which profit objectives are built in. Sometimes titled product manager, especially in USA.

Classified Salesman sells classified advertising on behalf of a newspaper or other publication. See also Tele-Ad Salesman.

Copywriter is usually part of a creative team in an advertising agency. His special talent is in being able to take a selling message and to express this in a clear communicative manner in the form of advertising "copy".

Copy Chief is the head of a group of Copywriters, or the person in an advertising agency responsible for the quality and creativity of the copy produced.

Corporate Affairs Manager is a relatively new function concerned with the planned development of good relationships between an organization and all of its publics – customers, employees, suppliers, shareholders, local community and so on.

Creative Director is the person in an advertising agency who directs the creative team in the preparation of advertisements, commercials or other such material.

Customer Relations Manager (Officer or Executive) deals with enquiries and complaints from customers as well as contributing to the planned development of a good customer relations programme.

Desk Researcher extracts data and information from published sources, usually as a service to the marketing programme.

Display Manager commonly employed in retailing to control the exhibition or display of merchandise whether in store or in window.

Estimator is part of the selling team and deals specifically with the preparation of estimates or quotations to prospective customers, usually for tailor-made products or services. More usually found in industrial marketing rather than consumer.

Exhibition Manager is in overall charge of the creation, preparation and production of an exhibition or exhibition stand. Job can also extend into provision of other three-dimensional material such as display units.

Export Sales Manager is responsible for a company's sales in overseas markets. He will often head up directly to the Board, and will spend much of his time travelling abroad.

Field Researcher obtains information, facts, data and opinions by means of personal interviews or observation of people "in the field".

Field Sales Manager controls the activities of outside salesmen.

Home Sales Manager is responsible for Home Sales, for example, sales in the United Kingdom, as opposed to overseas sales.

House Magazine Editor edits the internal (employee) and/or external (customer) magazine published by an organization.

Information Officer is primarily concerned with the collection, publication and distribution of information about an organization and its activities. It is sometimes used to describe the function of Public Relations Officer or Press Officer.

Interviewer is usually concerned with market research operations in which information is gathered by personal interviews.

Marketing Communications Manager manages the entire function of marketing communications, usually encompassing advertising, sales promotion and public relations.

Marketing Executive (or Officer) handles some part of the operations of a marketing department. Often specializes in a particular function, area, or group of products.

Marketing Manager (or Director) is the most senior executive controlling the overall marketing activities of an organization. He also manages the marketing department, directing the staff and controlling their operations.

Marketing Services Manager is the executive in charge of all marketing services, that is all marketing functions other than direct selling.

Marketing/Market Research Manager (Officer or Executive) is the person in an organization charged with the task of initiating research and interpreting it. He will sometimes actually undertake research work, but more often commission some outside agency to carry out particular projects.

Media Buyer is the executive in an advertising agency, responsible for timely and economical purchasing of media time and space (readership or audience) to discharge the requirements of a client's media schedule.

Media Manager (or Director) heads up the media department of an advertising agency, covering the planning and buying functions as well as the routine administrative and clerical systems.

Media Planner is the executive in an advertising agency responsible for formulating plans involving all types of media in such a way as to enable a client to reach out to his potential market(s) with maximum efficiency and minimum expense.

Mechandiser is employed by a marketing company to put into effect merchandising activities at retail outlets or other sales points.

National Accounts Manager is a senior sales executive who handles the needs of the major or 'national' customers of a company.

National Sales Manager – See Home Sales Manager.

Order Clerk works in the sales department of a company where he receives orders, records them and initiates the various documentation necessary to progress them to final delivery and invoicing.

Print Manager can be employed by either an advertising agency or client company to initiate and implement printed matter such as sales literature.

Press Officer is responsible for maintaining good relations and communications between an organization and the media. He will issue press releases, hold press receptions and generally see to the maximization of editorial publicity. Not to be confused with a Public Relations Officer.

Promotion Manager – See Sales Promotion Manager.

Production Manager is the executive in an advertising agency who sees to the conversion of illustrations and copy into a reproductive form such as blocks, litho plates and typesetting.

Public Affairs Director (or Manager) – *See* Corporate Affairs Director.

Publicity Manager (Officer or Executive) – *See* Advertising Manager.

Public Relations Consultant is an independent public relations executive who handles the public relations needs of one or more clients.

Public Relations Counsellor is a relatively unusual practitioner who gives advice (or counselling) on public relations matters, but does not carry out the executive work necessary to implement such advice.

Public Relations Officer (Manager or Executive) is responsible for the initiation and implementation of a deliberate and planned public relations programme on behalf of an organization. He will use a whole range of media from exhibitions to advertising and editorial publicity, and will usually be concerned with maintaining communications with a variety of publics – customers, employees, shareholders, opinion formers and so on. Not to be confused with a Press Officer, although his duties may include those of a Press Officer.

Publisher in a publishing house is the chief executive on a particular publication, and has control of editorial, advertising and circulation functions.

Regional Sales Manager – *See* Area Sales Manager.

Research Manager (Officer or Executive) – *See* Market Research Manager.

Sales Assistant is employed in the sales office of a marketing company to provide the office back-up to a salesman or group of salesmen. He will issue quotations, send out information, and generally give an all round service to customers.

Sales Clerk – *See Order Clerk.*

Sales Engineer is a specialized salesman usually with a technical knowledge about the product and its application.

Salesman is concerned with maintaining face-to-face contact with customers with a view to securing their business and maintaining it.

Sales Manager (or Director) is the executive responsible for sales force management, directly through field sales managers or through branch or area organization. Often also controls some internal sales service, which may or may not include transport, credit, repair, maintenance or other services.

Sales Office Manager is the executive responsible for managing the sales office and, in particular, ensuring that the necessary back-up is provided to the sales force in using company resources efficiently, thus exerting maximum persuasional effect upon customers.

Sales Promotion Manager (Officer or Executive) is the person in a marketing company who is responsible for undertaking the sales promotion programme.

Sales Representation (or Executive) – *See* Salesman.

Sales Serviceman – See Sales Assistant.

Sales Service Manager specializes in providing service to customers, usually in the form of after-sales service.

Scriptwriter writes the commentary or dialogue for a film or commercial.

Service Engineer is a specialist who services products after they have been delivered and/or installed.

Space Representative (or Salesman) is a specialist salesman employed by a publisher to sell advertising space.

Supervisor (Sales, Research) is a title often used in sales or market research to indicate a function which controls the activities of a number of people, e.g., interviewers.

Systems Engineer is another but more specialized title for a Sales Engineer: in this case concerned with recommending to customers overall systems as opposed to just individual products.

Technical Representative – See Sales Engineer.

Tele-Ad Salesman sells advertising space using primarily the telephone to communicate with customers. Much used in classified advertising.

Telephone Salesman is more commonly encountered in the USA than the UK, but as the name implies is a salesman who sets about securing orders by means of telephoning rather than personal calls.

Traffic Manager is the person in an advertising agency who ensures that all jobs are properly planned, progressed and produced on time.

Traveller – See Salesman.

Typographer is a person, frequently but not always an employee of an advertising agency, who produces type layouts or type markups, i.e., accurate specifications from which a printer can carry out typesetting.

Visualizer is a designer responsible for producing visual ideas for the interpretation and executive of an advertising brief. Usually, not necessarily, an employee of an advertising agency.

Bibliography

There are of course very many books to choose from, and for this reason a small number only are indicated here, these being just a few which are both broad in coverage and introductory in subject matter.

Marjorie Harris, *How to Get a Job* (Institute of Personal Management, 1983).

R. Braithwaite & P.C. Schofield, *How to Recruit* (British Institute of Management).

N.A. Hart and J. O'Connor, *The Practice of Advertising*, (Heinemann, 1983).

J. Stapleton, *Teach Yourself Marketing* (Hodder & Stoughton, 1984).

H. Lloyd, *Teach Yourself Public Relations* (Hodder & Stoughton, 1984).

Catherine Avent, *Which Career For You?* (Robert Hale, 1978).

Appendix: Careers Research

A survey was sent out to a small sample of employers in particular areas of marketing, advertising and public relations. They were asked to state the O-levels, A-levels and degrees they considered relevant for the variety of jobs that concerned them in their field of work. The results are shown in Table A.1. It should be noted that the first job title of the column is the short-term goal while the second one (in brackets) is the rather longer-term ambition.

The results themselves need a little explaining and commentary. It is important that they are taken as a *guideline* only. There are *no* six O-levels that should be taken to get into a specific job, neither are a certain three A-levels demanded by a particular job. The survey is intended to act as a pointer only.

The survey is highly subjective and represents the views of individuals (albeit very senior people) who gave their own choices for O-levels, A-levels and degrees. There is therefore the drawback that, as the information is entirely based on personal experience, full justice has not been given to those examinations that are relatively new or fairly specialized. For example, the survey shows that an economics degree is preferred by the employers in certain jobs but the term economics could well be meant to include related subjects, such as business studies.

It should be noted too that a list of three A-levels and a suggested degree does not mean that these examinations *ought* to be taken at all. Some of the respondents pointed out that a degree was not the best possible course of action and that experience often counted for a lot more. It might for instance be more useful to study a course that is related to the job you are doing, or intend to do, rather than take a degree.

While there are obvious disadvantages with the survey, there is one prominent advantage — it gives the student at least some basis to work on. Marketing, advertising and public relations functions are difficult to give specific careers advice on because of their diverse nature as they are relatively new, there is not yet any generally accepted career path either in experience or qualifications. Young people who are aged 14 and upwards often face the difficult choice of which O-levels and later which A-levels or degree they should take for their chosen career but so often they lack guidance. To be a doctor the examination choice is relatively simple, but to enter a world where there is no specific course to take will make decision-making difficult. This survey will give a form of guidance, although it is the individual who must make the choice in the end.

The following facts seemed to emerge from the research:

1 Qualifications, on the whole, were not all that important, and certainly came second place to such personal characteristics as drive, energy, ambition, lively mind, and so on.
2 For a number of larger companies, and particularly for management training schemes a degree was necessary, but the subject was unimportant.
3 Contrary to 2 above, for certain small companies a degree might be regarded as a disadvantage, particularly if the job being offered (e.g. a junior sales clerk) was thought by the employer to be below the level acceptable to a graduate.
4 At O-level, English language appears to be favoured by all, to which can be added English literature and a foreign language.
5 Economics seems to find general favour at all levels of study, and this can probably be interpreted as covering all business related studies.
6 For most jobs mathematics is regarded as desirable at O-level, as is sociology.

Job Title — Suggested Academic Qualifications

Table A.1

Brand Manager (Marketing Manager):

O Levels	Economics, English Language, English Literature, Foreign Language, History, Mathematics
A Levels	Economics, English, Mathematics
Degree	Economics

Salesman (Sales Manager):

O Levels	Economics, English Language, English Literature, Foreign Language, Mathematics, Sociology
A Levels	Economics, English, Mathematics
Degree	Economics/Business Studies

Account Executive (Account Director):

O Levels	Economics, English Language, English Literature, Foreign Language, Mathematics, Sociology
A Levels	Economics, English, Foreign Language/Mathematics
Degree	Economics

Copywriter (Creative Director):

O Levels	Art, English Language, English Literature, Foreign Language, History, Sociology
A Levels	Art, English, Economics/History/Sociology
Degree	English

PRO (PR Manager):

O Levels	Economics, English Language, English Literature, Foreign Language, History, Sociology
A Levels	Economics, English, Sociology
Degree	English/Business Studies

Visualizer (Creative Director):

O Levels	Art, English Language, English Literature, Geography, History, Sociology
A Levels	Art, English, Sociology
Degree	Art

Media Planner/Buyer (Media Director):

O Levels	Economics, English Language, Foreign Language, Geography, Mathematics, Sociology
A Levels	Economics, English, Mathematics
Degree	Mathematics/Economics

Researcher (Research Director):

O Levels	Economics, English Language, English Literature, Mathematics, Science, Sociology
A Levels	Economics, Mathematics, Sociology/Statistics
Degree	Economics

Table A.1 (continued)

Media Representative (Advertisement Manager):

O Levels	Economics, English Language, English Literature, Foreign Language, History, Mathematics
A Levels	Economics, English, Mathematics/Sociology
Degree	Economics

Advertising Executive (Advertising Manager):

O Levels	Economics, English Language, English Literature, Foreign Language, History, Mathematics
A Levels	Economics, English, Foreign Language
Degree	Economics

Index